VOLUME 3

DAYTON, TENNESSEE NEWSPAPERS

ISSUES FROM 1904 AND 1907

Compiled
by
Bettye J. Broyles

Rhea County Historical and Genealogical Society

Heritage Books
2024

HERITAGE BOOKS

AN IMPRINT OF HERITAGE BOOKS, INC.

Books, CDs, and more—Worldwide

For our listing of thousands of titles see our website
at
www.HeritageBooks.com

A Facsimile Reprint
Published 2024 by
HERITAGE BOOKS, INC.
Publishing Division
5810 Ruatan Street
Berwyn Heights, MD 20740

Published by
The Rhea County Historical and Genealogical Society

2001

International Standard Book Number
Paperbound: 978-0-7884-8738-5

FOREWORD

Although Volume 3 of the Rhea County newspapers includes only four issues, they contain a tremendous amount of information about the county and her inhabitants.

The January 1904 issue of *The Enterprise* (Volume II, No. 52), edited by W.W. Shields, covers a vaiety of subjects, including articles on the need for better pay for teachers and a county high school, local happenings, a report from the County Court, a directory for Dayton and the county, lists of Fraternities and Churches, a dead letter list from the Post Office, and numerous advertisements used in the newspaper. This issue was copied from a microfilm obtained from the State Archives.

In June of 1904, on the sixth anniversary of the *Weekly Herald* (Vol. VII, No. 1), Editor T.J. Campbell published a 16-page issue containing many articles on the history of Rhea County, her progress, and sketches of many of the men who contributed to the county's history. The outside sheet (pages 1,2,15, and 16) were copied from the State Archives microfilm, but the remaining pages are among the files of the Rhea County Historical Society.

As a word of caution, some of the statements in the histories written by W.L. Givens, V.C. Allen, and H.A. Crawford, have since been shown to be incorrect or cannot be proved; therefore, please consult the *History of Rhea County, Tennessee*, published in 1991 by the Historical Society, for additional information.

By 1907, one Dayton newspaper had changed its name from *The Enterprise* to *The Republican Enterprise* (Vol. XIII, No. 31), but it was still being edited by W.W. Shields. The high school was still a topic, as was the Richmond Hosiery Mill, and the monthly Teacher's Association meeting. Many citizens were mentioned in the Local Personal column, which requested "If Your Friends Come or Go, Die or Marry, Let Us Know It." The issue also gives an account of the settlement of the estate of Mrs. B.G. Pyott by V.C. Allen, and a list of unclaimed County warrants. A complete roster of the officers for the County and the City of Dayton were also included.

The Weekly Herald (Vol. X, No. 14), still edited by T.J. Campbell, as well as *The Republican Enterprise*, reported on the scandal involving the Baptist Church. The "Bits of Local Information" in The Herald records the coming and going of citizens and visitors to the county. An article on Rhea Springs mentions the Conferate Veterans Reunion and another article explains the origin of southern the phrase "You All." One article discusses Domestic Science as taught in the schools.

Most of the advertisements from all four newspapers have also been included since they reveal the various businesses in the county and the type of goods they carried or services they were engaged in.

Bettye J. Broyles

CONTENTS

THE ENTERPRISE
[7 January 1904]

THE ENTERPRISE.

DAYTON, TENNESSE, THURSDAY, JANUARY 7, 1904.

VOL. II   NO. 52.

Subscription $1 PER YEAR In Advance

Done Neatly and Promptly

BETTER SCHOOLS

STIRRING APPEAL TO THE COUNTY COURT FOR MORE FUNDS FOR THE PUBLIC SCHOOLS, REACHES THE HEARTS OF OUR COUNTY SOLONS. EXCELLENT PA...

KALHOUN KROSS

THE ENTERPIRSE.

Weekly published in the best interests of Dayton and Rhea county. : : : :

W. W. SHIELDS, Editor & Prop

Entered in at the Postoffice of Dayton Tenn., as second-class mail matter.

Subscription, $1.00 per year in Advance

All communications for publication should reach this office not later than Wednesday of each week; also the name of writer should accompany each ms., not for punblication but as a guarantee of good faith.

Correspodence Solicited,

BETTER SCHOOLS

STIRRING APPEAL TO THE COUNTY COURT FOR MORE FUNDS FOR THE PUBLIC SCHOOLS, REACHES THE HEARTS OF OUR COUNTY SOLONS. EXCELLENT PAPER READ BEFORE THAT BODY BY MISS LENA MORGAN, OF MORGANTOWN.

Mr. Chairman and Members of the County Court:

We, the teachers of Rhea County, beseech you to lend us a listening ear. We come before you as suppliants to a higher power, and so great is our confidence in your superior wisdom and in your zeal in the faithful discharge of every known duty that if we can but bring you to a realization of the pressing needs of the schools of Rhea County, we feel assured that our purpose will be accomplished.

We teachers are in a position to understand the gravity of the situation better than you do, better even than the patrons of our schools do.

Were the parents of the school children of this county sensible of the vital importance of our request they would fill this court room to overflowing, and our petition would elicit from them a most hearty amen.

What we ask for is an increased school fund in order that we may have a longer term of school and better paid teachers.

In a term of three or four months such as we usually have in our county, a student can do little more than accomodate himself to his surroundings and get his mind into proper training for study. Then he leaves school and spends the remaining eight or nine months in idleness. The next year he returns and takes up his work — not where he dropped it — but on account of his retrogression, almost where he began it the previous year.

Thus it is, year after year, and as a consequence mental advancement of the children is so slow, we teachers are often unjustly charged with incompetence. That teacher, pray, could accomplish much under existing circumstances. `

We admit that some of our profession are not as well qualified as they should be, but will you not in return acknowledge that in many of our schools the term is so short and the salary is so small that you yourselves wonder that those schools are supplied with teachers.

No teacher who is thoroughly equipped for his profession, whose soul is in his work, can be content to teach only a few months of the year. Both his desire for remuneration commensurate with his ability and his enthusiasm in the cause of education demands a longer service.

Therefore if you want the standard of the teachers of Rhea County raised, give us an eight or nine months term of school all over the county, and larger salaries in some of the rural schools, and you will have arrived at a happy solution of the problem.

You may object to this proposition adducing as your reason the financial inability of the county to levy an additional tax, for school purposes. We are aware of the fact, however, that our county is practically out of debt; yet were this not the case you could not afford to act niggardly in this matter.

You pay the convicts forty cents a day, making a salary of $140 a year; while the avarage salary of the school teachers of Rhea County is $186 a year. We ask you, is it just to make this difference between an element on the one hand that is trying to drag our county to destruction, and a profession, on the other hand, that is striving to uplift humanity?

Furthermore, we wish to call your attention to the fact that of the present school levy of $5898.31 the C.S. Railroad pays $3419.56; the Western Union Telegraph Co. $20.02; the East Tenn. Telephone Co. $18.20; the Gainesboro Telephone Co. $2.16; and the Meigs Co. $.54, making a total of $3455.48; thus leaving you to pay only $2442.88. Will you permit these corporations which are indirectly interested in the welfare of our county to contribute more than you do to the liberation of our citizenship from the tralldom of ignorance?

Ex-Gov. Crittenden of Ky. wisely said: "Parsimony toward education is liberality toward crime." Since in proportion to our advancement in education there is a corresponding decrease of crime would it not be expedient for you to appropriate more money to the public school fund, and thereby be compelled to spend less in the support of criminals?

We are forced to admit the truth of Edward Everett's assertion. "Education is a better safeguard of liberty than a standing army. If we retrench the wages of the school-master, we must raise those of the recruiting officer."

Equally sure are we that Benjamin Harrison spoke truly when he said, "I have a firm belief that the rock of our safety as a nation lies in the proper education of our population."

Where are found the people that contribute nothing to the progress and prosperity of our civilization? Among the uncultured.

Whither shall we turn to find the element that is devoid of the moral stamina to resist the

3

influence of agitators of lawlessness? To the un-educated.

From whence come the men and women, who being dominated by the baser passions commit crimes too horrible to be dwelt upon? We reply from the illiterate class.

Our worthy county superintendent, Mr. Fred B. Frazier, is inspired by an ambition to crush this monster illiteracy by making the schools of Rhea county second to those of no other county in Tenn., or in any other state. Then is he to be thwarted in his noble aim by your refusal to place at his disposition a sufficient amount of money?

Are the children of Rhea county, your children and your neighbor's children — to be deprived of a common school education, the heritage of every child of America, because of a lack of cooperation on the part of you who are in authority? Are the boys and girls of today, who will be the men and women of tomorrow to be launched on a career of vice and crime because gross inattention to this burning question? Surely not. We confidently believe that your patriotism which manifested itself during the stormy days of the sixties will characterize you no less in the defense of the youth of our county against their most relentless enemy — ignorance.

We now feel emboldened to ask you for an increase of ten cents on the hundred dollars taxable property to be applied to the public school fund. Since the taxable property of our county is $3,116,514 this proposed increase would give us $3,116.51, a sum so requisite to the materialization of our plans for a thorough education and a higher plane of life for the boys and girls of Rhea county.

Feeling that we have won your sympathy and that you will not turn us away empty handed, we read to you our resolutions which were adopted by the Rhea County Teacher's Institute at its December session.

"Resolved that we favor the increase of school funds for Rhea county for the following reasons: Because the present available school funds fall far short of meeting the needs in any and all the school districts in the county: (1) as to length of term; (2) as to suitable and comfortable school buildings, furniture and fixtures; (3) as to sufficiency to command and hold the best and most efficient teaching service. It is entirely insufficient to permit anything like efficient work in grading school — a thing so essential to progress in school work. By grading schools, pupils have so much to accomplish each year and the next year they move on to higher and more difficult work. Thus having a goal, incentives are furnished that result in satisfactory progress.

Resolved, therefore, that we favor an additional levy for school purposes by county court of ten cents on the hundred dollars taxable property of the county. Be it further resolved that we favor the adoption of one or more county High Schools for Rhea county, and request the committee appointed for that purpose to call the court's attention to this fact.

The trustees of the Confederate Soldiers' Home have elected Mr. Sumner Kirkpatrick of Nashville to be superintendent of the Home, and he will assume his duties tomorrow. Mr. Kirkpatrick is a native of Sumner county, but has lived in Nashville since his youth.

Alaska now supplies half the salmon of the world.

Over 400,000 people in London live in single room tenements.

The amount paid in pensions since the civil war is $8,134,271,548.

About one tenth of the voters in Boston and Chicago are socialites.

The total expenditure for the navy for the next fiscal year is $102,866,443.

KALHOUN KROSS

WRITTEN FOR THE ENTERPRISE
POSSUM CREEK 10SC, 9 TEEN & 3

In each number of the News of Chattanooga, yule find "Stories of the town" and from the tone hiz voice, and a long ackwaintance ime of oponion that theze very interestin letters are written by Henry M. Wiltse; there iz plun and information in each of theze articles but I started out to notice only one of theze in which the riter makes the statements that on a certain lovely day in that town a man deskivered certain pheuomenon of the sun not heretofore noticed by him I do not remember the Xact langwidge and thereto give the statements in my own; it waz to the effect that the sun had a curdled or mottled appearance az thos sufferein from billiousness and marked there and there by long streaks of light called facula which look like foam fleaks below a kataract, with spots on it that vary from minute pores the size of an ordinary skool districk to spots a hundred thousand miles visible to the nude eye; the center of theze spots iz az black az a brunett cat and are kalled the urabra bekase they so much resemble the umberella, the next cirkle iz less dark and iz kalled the penumbra; because it resembles the penumbra, there are many theories regarding theze spots, but to be perfectly kandid with the gentle reader, neither professor Bill Benson not myself kan tell Xactly what they are; if we could get a little kloser perhaps we cud speak more definitely; mi own theory Xpressed in a crude way iz that they are open air kaukuses held by the colored people of the sun, or that they may be the dark hosses in the kampaign; or they may be the spots knocked ofen the defeated kandidate i the kampaign by the opposition; frankly however i dont believe that either of theze theories iz ten-able; Prof. Fate Lillard skoffs at theze theories also on the ground that theze spots do not revolve az fast az the sun, this, however, ime prepared to Xplain upon the theory that this

mout be the result of "delays in the returns"; with all its pekularities, the sun iz a great thing for this old yeth; we owe much of our enjoyment to the sun, and if it shud go somewhere for a phew weeks for relaxation and rest it wud be a cold day for us, its the great source of light and heat; the moon wud be useless, for she iz largely dependent on the sun; animal life wud soon cease with the sun and real estate wud bekum depressed; not many years ago a large number of people worshiped the sun; when a man showed symtons of emotional in-sanity, they took him up on the observatory of the Temple and sacrificed him to the sun; they were a very prosperous and happy people and if the konqueror hadnt kum among them with civilization and guns and grand Juries they wud have kontinued very happy; indeed ive known people who worried a heap for fear the sun wud cease to draw a salary and make an asignment; some think that the chances are good for a large comet to plow into the sun some dark rainy night and bust up the whole yuniverse; i wish that waz all i had to worry about, if any respectable man will agree to pay mi taxes and phuneral Zpenses, ile agree to do hiz worryin about the comet krashin into the sun and knockin its day lights out; ive studied the komet, and believe if we cud get klose to it, without frightenin it away, wede find that we cud walk through it any where az we cud thru the glare of a torch light procession; however, we shud so live that wele not be ashamed to look a comet in the eye; LET US PAY UP OUR NEWS PAPER SUBSCRIPTION, and lead sich lives that when the comet strikes wele be ready; one riter haz sed, of a comet, that the substance of the nebuosity and the tale iz of almost inkonceivable temerity; he sed this and then death kame to hiz relief; an other riter says of the comet and its tail that the curvature of the latter, and the accelernation of the perodic time in the kase of Enkea comet indikate their bein effected by a resistin medium which haz never been observed to have the slightest influence on the planetary periods; i do not fully agree with the eminent authority tho he may be right; much fear haz bin the result of the comits appearance ever since the world began, and its az good a thing to worry about az i no of. 4 hundred years ago, a scientist diskivered that comets were attaneous to our klimate, and since then time has improved; i kan see that trade iz better and taters run less to the toes; no other one diskivered a bout the same time, that comets all had more or less periodicity; no one node how they got it astronomers had bin watchin them but did not kno when they were Xposed but there were over 3 hundred of them al down with it at once; tother day i met Col Gardenhire and sed how professor i found a bran new star, and intend to file it. i found it runin loose between the zenith and ten o'clock at night, havent heard of any body losing a star of the fiftenth magnitude, with light mane and tail have ye? and this star was about thirteen hands high sed he; when i konsulted N.D. Reed's star katalogue new and second hand ones, i do not find any sich star loose.

The associated Press in announcing the death of Gen. James A. Longstreet was in error in stating that he left only one other living lieutenant-general of the Cofederate army. The fact is there are three left, and many claim there are four. Gen. Simon Bolivar Buckner, of Kentucky, is now the ranking lieutenant-general left, Gen. A.P. Stewart of this city next, then Gen. Stephen D. Lee of Mississippi, and it is claimed that Gen. Joe Wheeler held that rank when the war closed.— Chattanooga Times

----

The balance in the state treasury at the close of the year is $307,813.80. The sinking fund for December amounts to $3,483.46. The receipts for 1903 were $2,862,481.77 and disbursements $2,423,292.63. The balance on hand Jan. 1, 1903, was $439,197.14.

[page 2]

THE KID'S HOME-COMING.

BY MARGUERITE STABLER.

JUDICIAL DIGNITY

Was Maintained in This Instance At Cost to the Court of the Prisoner

----

A certain squire of the city, who betrays his patriotism by presiding in a small office painted red, wbite and blue, had a case before him the other day which attracted an unusual crowd to the temple of justice. A young fellow was up before him, relates the Pittsburg Dispatch, on a charge of stealing brass, and his friends were out in full force to see that he got a fair show.

Before the case opened the noise and confusion became so great that his honor declared that the next man to indulge in any unusual outbreak would be ejected from the room. He had hardly ceased speaking when a young man shouted, at the same time waving his hat above his head:

"Hooray for Squire Hooligan!"

"Put him out," roared the court, and in another instant the young man found himself being rushed to the door. Order having been restored once more, his honor ordered that the prisoner be brought before the bar for trial. The court officer hurriedly glanced about through the crowd and then a great light suddenly fell upon him.

"Can't do it your honor," he replied. "The young fellow you just put out was the prisoner."

THE "400" AND THE ZOO

An Alliance Which Some Persons Were Consummately Ignorant About

----

"Some people," said the Philadelphia woman, according to a New York exchange, "have a queer idea of what the '400' does, and it does queer things, goodness known, without having things it doesn't do laid to it.

"I was going through the zoo the other day with a friend," she went on, "and while we were standing before a cage in the lion house my companion turned to me and asked:

" 'I wonder who keeps all this up?'

"Before I had a chance to reply, we were both astonished to hear a deep Irish voice reply:

" 'Sure, madam, it's the society.'

"We turned and beheld as healthy a looking specimen of the working woman as ever I laid eyes on.

" 'The society?' questioned my companion, in a half amused way. 'What society?'

"The washerwoman looked us all over with contempt; then she blurted out:

" 'The society — the society! What ninnies ye are! Sure, an' haven't ye ever heard of the '400' — the society of Noo York? That's the society that keeps this here place up!'

"And with that she turned on her heel and left we two ignoramuses staring in blank amazement after her retreating bulk."

Dish Washing in Winter

Housekeepers naturally dread dish washing in winter, owing to the fact that it chaps the hands and renders them hard and rough. Much of the injury, however, results from the use of impure soap. If Ivory soap is used in washing dishes and the hands are carefully rinsed and dried, they will not chap.

ELEANOR R. PARKER

Young Salt — "How's the fish bitin' today, uncle?"

Old Salt — "With their mouths, as usual, youngster." — Harvard Lampoon.

Stops the Cough

and works off the cold. Laxative Bromo Quinine Tablets. Price 25 cents.

Reward of Economy

Kwoter — What's that old saying? 'Take care of the pennies and — "

Newitt — And the dollars will take care of your heirs. — Philadelphia Press.

The richest purse often has the poorest contents. — Town Topics.

June Tint Butter Color makes top of the market butter.

Virtue and happiness are twin sisters. — Chicago Daily News

Significant

Margaret's father and mother, whose home was in New York City, had arranged to take a long talked of trip to Chicago. The night before they were to start on their western expedition Margaret's mamma told the little girl that she must go to bed early, as she would have to be up by daylight the next morning.

Margaret very obediently consented to prepare for bed. When her dress had been taken off and her nightie put on, she knelt to say her prayers. She closed her petition as follows:

"Good-by, God! Good-by, angels! Good-by! Good-by! I'm going to Chicago tomorrow!" — Woman's Home Companion.

Glad Caller

Mistress — Did anyone call while I was out, Jane?

Jane — Yis, mum. Wan gintlemin wus afther callin', mum.

"What was his name?"

"Moik O'Rafferty, mum, an' he wus as glad to foind yez out as he wus to foind me in. Oi'm thinkin', mum." — Chicago Daily News

----

[Page 3]

Local Happenings.

Reader, if you are not already a subscriber to the Enterprise, we send you this copy to invite you to become one, and to acquaint you with the new plans, purposes and prospects of the paper. It is your paper. Tell your neighbors about it. Send us their subscription. Send us the news of your neighborhood. Come to see us when you are in town and use your influence to make of The Enterprise a better newspaper than we have ever planned.

The Mississippi Legislature has, by an almost unanimous vote, instructed its U.S. senators to vote for the ratification of the Panama treaty, following the example of the legislature of other southern states. The south is determined to have the canal; and if the democratic leaders presist in their present course of obstruction, they may soon be inquiring, "Can the democrats Carry Mississippi?"

Joe Vasey, district board member U.M.W. of A. and Mr. Sarley of Alabama, addressed a large mass meeting at the court house Thursday night on the labor problem. They are both among the leading labor leaders of the south and while they are strong union men, they urge conservatism.

They are entertaining speakers and thoroughly understand the problems at issue.

News has been received in the city today of the total destruction by fire of James R. Darwin's handsome residence at Circle, Meigs County. Mr. Darwin was formerly a citizen of Dayton, and has many friends here who will regret to learn of his misfortune, his home was one of the most comfortable and nicely finished in Meigs county.

Mr. George West, one of Rhea County's most prominent citizens and attorneys, is in Athens spending a few days with his parents, Mr. and Mrs. T.R. West. — Athenian-Citizen

Pat Haughey, a former popular business man of Dayton, now of Chattanooga, was among friends in this city Monday. While here he was entered as the first 1904 subscriber to The Enterprise.

Push said the button.
Never be led said the pencil.
Take pains, said the window.
Always keep cool, said the ice.
Be up to date, said the calender.
Do business on tick, said the clock.
Never lose your head, said the barrel.
Never do anything off hand, said the glove.
Doing a driving business, said the hammer.
Be sharp in all your dealings, said the knife.
Trust to your stars success, said the night.
Spend much time in reflection, said the mirror.
Make much of small things, said the microscope.
Strive to make a good impression, said the seal.
Find a good thing and stick to it, said the glue.
Turn all things to your advantage, said the lathe.
Make the most of your good points, said the compass.

The D.C. & I. Co., beginning the first of the year, cut all employee's wages 10 per cent.

Q. & C. agent Taylor has gone to Florida to spend the winter and Sam Nelson has succeeded him; while J.C. Jennings takes Mr. Nelson's place at the North Dayton depot.

W.C. Baily has resigned as administrator and Judge Foust qualified as guardian for Franklin's heirs.

Ike Holloman is visiting friends in Chattanooga.

The Black Haw medicine Co. is installing a new power printing press, with G.T. Proxmire as foreman.

Roy Reynolds after spending the holidays with his parents returned to Philadelphia, Pa., Tuesday.

Capt. Webb Thomas gave us a pleasant visit Tuesday. The Capt. is a veteran newspaper man and an interesting talker.

Mr. and Mrs. Ern Moore have returned from an extensive visit with relatives at Grief.

Ruth, oldest daughter of Ex-President Cleveland, died Wednesday.

Gen. John B. Gordon is reported to be dying at Miami, Florida.

John Mathis, of Waldensia, is visiting in the city.

The Chattanooga News offers grand prizes to the four most popular young ladies in its territory outside of Chattanooga. Which young lady of Dayton will get one of these valuable prizes?

Will Morgan, Bob Gillespie, John Crawford and ----- [blank] Kelly have gone to Maryville to enter college.

Mr. Human, of Harriman, general agent for the Singer Machine company, is in the city.

Richard Baskett called on Spring City friends Sunday.

The city school opened Tuesday with bright prospects for a successful year. Prof. Fooshee and faculty are building up the school and making it one worthy of the most liberal patronage.

COUNTY COURT

County Court met Monday, chairman Leuty presiding and Justices Henry, Lillard, Dodd, Darwin, Brady and White present.

W.T. Gass, J.B. Swafford, V.C. Allen, J.C. Dodd and W.L. Lillard were appointed a committee to draft resolutions on the death of the late 'Squire M.B. Hicks.

Dr. W.B. Williams was granted an appropriation of $271 for attending smallpox and $28 for attending patients in jail.

J. L. Henry was unanimously elected chairman.

Dr. J.R. Gillespie unanimously elected county physician.

Road commissioners were elected as follows:

1st district —	James Foust
2nd district —	J. A. Torbutt [sic]
3rd district —	W. A. Templeton
4th district —	W.Y. Denton
Coroner —	J.A. Whitner

Poorhouse commissioner, 8 years: Y.F. Shaver

Notaries public: V.C. Allen, J.W. Clouse, L.L. Barton, John Harwood, Dave Harvey.

The Revenue commission — W.E. Stephens, J.C. Nelson and T.N.L. Cunnyngham — made its report which was accepted.

$329.40 was appropriated to the poor house fund.

B.H. Myers, J.H. Hickman and W.Y. Denton were appointed a committee to ascertain the condition of the Sale Creek bridge.

Hon. W.B. Miller asked for an appropriation $170 for the "Hermitage" fund which was allowed.

A resolution to establish a county high school was unamously rejected (and Prof. Rogers wasn't there either).

$25 per month, for expenses, was appropriated to superintendent Frazier.

Judge B.G. McKenzie was employed as county attorney for 1904.

The following tax levy was made:

.25 cents for county purposes.

.05 cents for Poor House.

.22 cents for Bridges.

.10 cents for Roads.

.15 cents for special Judgments, etc.

Poll tax $2.00 or five days on roads.

RURAL ROUTE EXAMINATION

Rural route inspector Graham inspected the proposed new routes leading out of Dayton Wednesday and Thursday. One route goes out by Ogden to New Harmony and back by Morgan Springs; the other goes up the valley via Evensville to Clear Creek and back by Washington.

Mr. Graham will recommend the establishment of these routes. He is holding an examination for carriers today. Messers R.J. Harvey, A.J. Thacker, J.D. Patton, W.A. Dodd, Pete Talent, T.W. Knight, W.A. Knight, and J.C. Turner are taking the examination.

ADVERTISEMENTS FROM PAGE 3

[Page 4]

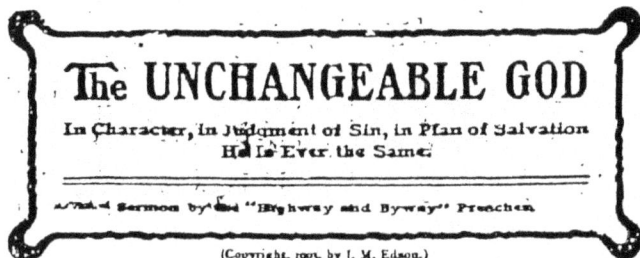

The UNCHANGEABLE GOD

In Character, in Judgment of Sin, in Plan of Salvation He Is Ever the Same.

A 2nd Sermon by the "Highway and Byway" Preacher.

(Copyright, 1903, by J. M. Edson.)

MISCELLANEOUS ITEMS

A judge of a court of record is held, in Webb vs Fisher (Tenn.), 60 L.R.A. 79, not to be subject to a private action for oppressively, maliciously and corruptly entering a decree disbarring an attorney.

The steepest mountain railway in Europe is being built from the Tryolean village of Kalten to the Mendel pass. Its gradient is 64 degrees, thus excelling that of the Stranserhorn in Switzerland, which has heretofore held the record.

An interesting scheme has been launched with the view of alleviating the misery caused by the failure of the sardine fisheries off the coast of Brittany. It consists in the emigration of the Breton fishermen to the shores of Algiers and Tunis, where the fish is so abundant that one Sicilian fleet of 2,500 boats employs over 12,000 men.

Already several hundred Breton families have handed in their names at various towns and villages; but danger of the scheme failing lies in the absorbing love of country, for nearly all the fishermen make the condition that they shall be brought back to spend the clore [sic] season in their native haunts.

ADVERTISEMENT FROM PAGE 4

Business Precaution

A caller at the boarding house of Mrs. Irons was surprised to see a fine greyhound basking in the sun outside the kitchen door. "I didn't know you had a dog," she said. "He's a beautiful animal. How long have you had him?"

"Two or three years."

"How does it happen I have never seen him in passing along here?"

"We don't allow him to leave the back yard," replied Mrs. Irons, with emphasis. "What kind of an advertisement would it be for a boarding house to have a creature as lean as that dog is standing round in front of it?" — Youth's Companion.

Cheap Notoriety

Mrs. Closefist — Oh, do buy me a new bonnet, my dear. It will set all my friends talking.

Mr. Closefist — If you're after notoriety, why don't you get the old one retrimmed? That will make your friends talk twice as much. — Stray Stories.

"Some folks," said Uncle Eben, "gits credit foh bein' lucky 'case dey has sense; an' others gits credit foh havin' sense 'cause dey's lucky." Washington Star.

[Page 5]

SMILES IN THE RAIN

The coward may smile
When there's sun all the while —
    It's braver to smile in the rain.
The weakest may joy
When there's naught to annoy —
    He's stronger who smiles through his pain.
An then when there's sun, when there's bird song
      and breeze,
When gloom's put to rout, and discouragement
      flees,

What need has the world
Of the mouth corners curled
In the cheeriest smiles, when the fields and trees
Are smiling so broadly that nobody sees
The wee bit of brightness you're giving the
      while?
But days when it's rainy there's need for your
      smile.

The weakling may smile
When there's brightness the while —
    It's better to smile when there's rain;
The gloomaster may joy
When there's naught to annoy —
    He's brave who can laugh through his pain.
When all the world is so full of song
That birds sing and brooklets go warbling along;
With hearts light as chaff
All the earth seems to laugh —
The sunny day courage says not you are strong.
Through hearty good cheer one could never call
      wrong —
But oh, when the day is all haggard and gray
And nature weeps gloomily, sobbing away —
Then laugh in the hope of the sweet afterwhile;
On days when it's rainy there's need for your
      smile.

    [by] S.W. Gillian, in Baltimore American

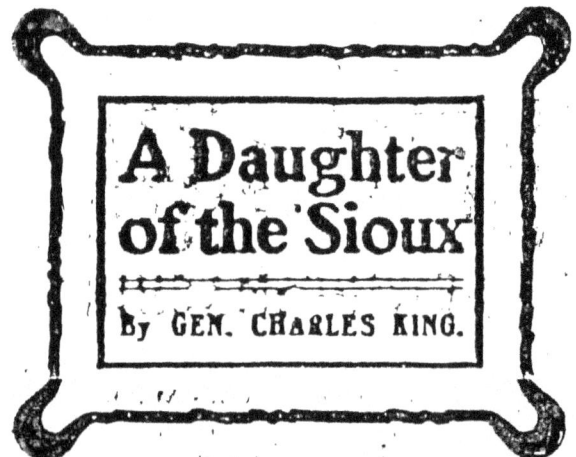

A Daughter of the 'Sioux'

by GEN. CHARLES KING.

Copyright, 1902, by The Hobart Company.

How "General Joe" Dwindled

Everybody knows General Joe Wheeler, former Lieutenant General C.S.A., at present Major General of the United States army (retired), and between times representative in congress from Alabama, is a man of quality rather than of quantity, and one seeing him can scarcely understand how so small a body has been able to fill so much space in the world's history of achievement, says the New York Times.

One day during his congressional career two rural visitors were in the house gallery taking in the proceedings on the floor with great interest, and one of them observed the general flying about, as was his wont.

"Who's that little cuss down there in front talkin' to the big feller?" he asked of his companion.

"Dinged if I know," replied the other, squinting his eyes in order to magnify the object of vision.

Some one sitting back of them ventured the information that it was Gen. Wheeler, of Alabama.

"My gravy!" said the first one, "I've heard that a feller might be a good deal of a man at home, but when he was elected to congress and come to Washington he fell off some and wasn't much of a heavyweight, but I'll be derned if I thought they'd dwindle away like that."

Who Licked Great Britain

Senator Aldrick, of Rhode Island, visited a typical music hall, the last time he was abroad, says the New York Tribune. A one-act melodrama called "The British Heart of Oak" was played by seven men and a young woman. The time of the melodrama was laid in the early years of the last century, and four of the players represented American soldiers.

These American soldiers were a ragged, scarcrow lot, for it was the idea of the melodrama to ridicule the American army. As the men came on the stage they were put through an examination.

"What was your business before you became a soldier?" they would be asked, and to this question, one answered that he had been a tailor, another that he had been a cobbler, and a third that he had been a cook, and so on.

The audience laughed uproariously at an army composed of men from such sedentary and confining trades, but in the midst of the laughter Senator Aldrick's American heart was rejoiced to hear a voice shout from the gallery:

"Hurray! Great Britain licked by tailors, cobblers, and cooks! Hurray!"

Disillusionized

Some officers of a British ship were dining with a mandarin at Canton, says the New York News. One of the guests wished for a second helping of a savory stew, which he thought was some kind of duck, and not knowing the word in Chinese, held his plate to the host, saying, with smiling approval:

"Quack, quack, quack!"

His countenance fell when his host, pointing to the dish, responded:

"Bow, wow, wow!"

"Oh, for the wings of a dove!" sighed the poet with the unbarbered hair. "Order what you like," rejoined the prosaic person, "but as for me, give me the breast of a chicken."—Chicago News

----

[Page 6]

DIRECTORY

---o---

CITY OF DAYTON

Mayor	R. M. Sherman
Clerk and Recorder	P. T. Foust
Marshall	W. J. Lowery
Aldermen	Joe Morgan, J.L. Daniel, Dr. J. Thomison, William White, E. P. Johnson, Arch Rollins, J.A. Denton

RHEA COUNTY

---o---

Chairman County Court	J. L. Henry
Clerk " "	W. B. Kelly
Sheriff	N. J. Tallent
Trustee	J. W. Vance
Circuit Court Clerk	W. B. Allen
Clerk and Master	T. J. Gillespie
Coroner	J. A. Whitener
Supt. of Education	Fred B. Frazier
Register	E. Fisher
Election Commissioners	E. T. Waterhouse,
	H. C. Torbut, H. Benson

COURTS

---o---

CHANCERY — meets First Monday in February and August — Hon. T.M. McConnell, Chancellor.

CIRCUIT — meets Second Tuesday in April, August and December — Hon. J.E. Higgins, Judge; W.W. Fairbanks, Attorney General.

COUNTY — meets First Monday in --?-- [line too blurred to read]

CHURCHES

FIRST BAPTIST — Rev. G.W. Brewer pastor. Preaching every Sunday at 11 a.m. and 7 p.m. Sunday School 9:30 a.m. Prayer meeting Wednesday at 7 p.m. Ladies' Aid Society Wednesday evenings 2:30 o'clock.

SECOND BAPTIST — Rev. J.M. Manning, pastor. Preaching Second Saturday and Sunday evenings at 7:30. Sunday School 10 a.m.

M.E. CHURCH — Rev. W.C. Wheeler, pastor. Preaching every Sunday at 7 o'clock p.m. Sunday School at 9:30 a.m. Prayer meeting Thursday 7 p.m. Junior League 3 p.m. Epworth League 2 p.m.

M.E. CHURCH SOUTH — Rev. Frank Y. Jackson. Preaching every Sunday 11 a.m. and 7 p.m. Sunday School 9:30 a.m. Prayer meeting Wednesday evening 7:30. Junior League 7:30 p.m.

PRESBYTERIAN — Rev. W.H. Covert, pastor. Preaching every Sunday at 11 a.m. Sunday School 9:30 a.m.

CHURCH OF CHRIST — Services every Sunday conducted by Dr. J. R. Hoover at 11 o'clock a.m. Sunday School 10 a.m.

CATHOLIC CHURCH — Services at 7 o'clock a.m. by Father Racier, Fourth Sundays; Sunday School every Sunday at 3 p.m.

FRATERNITIES

---o---

MASONIC — Dayton Lodge 572 F & A.M. meets First Monday in each month at 7 p.m. A.J. Clark, W.M.; W.L. Lillard, Sec.; John Morgan, Treasurer.

I.O.O.F. — Dayton Lodge No. 21 meets each Tuesday evening. W.R. Presnell, N.G., J.S. Young, Sec.

KNIGHTS OF PYTHIAS — Hope Lodge No.57 meets every Friday evening. Visiting Knights cordially invited. F.E. Cunnyngham, O.G. B.B. Blevins, K.R.B.

U.M.W. of A. — Dayton Lodge, 1117, meets Saturday evening 7 o'clock. Henry Morgan, Pres., Eulus Wilson, Sect., John Senters, Treas.

ANNOUNCEMENT

As announced in our last week's issue in a card from Mr. W.A. Giboney, who for the past year has owned and published THE ENTERPRISE, that gentleman has sold all his interest in THE ENTERPRISE plant to local parties and has entirely severed his connection with the paper.

We are glad to be able to announce this week that the present proprietors expect to add new material and equipment to the office at an early date, by which improvements in the appearance of the paper will be possible.

In our next, or another early issue, we hope to be able to give the friends of The Enterprise some additional good news that we are not now allowed to divulge.

With better opportunities and advantages than here-to-fore enjoyed we shall redouble our efforts and renew our energies in our endeavor to give the people of Rhea county, into whose homes The Enterprise finds its way, a clean, attractive, readable and up-to-date newspaper brimful of the latest local and general news accurately, and impartially stated.

We shall discuss local questions of public importance vigorously and fearlessly with the best interest of the citizens and tax-payers as our only guiding star.

In politics THE ENTERPRISE will from this time forward, to the best of its ability, uphold the principles and policies of the republican party, firmly believing their establishment and maintenance to be necessary to the greatest growth and glory of our nation and to the highest happiness, contentment and prosperity of her people.

The Rhea county court can talk more and say less than any legislative body on earth.

The days of bossism in Rhea county have passed says The Herald. The hands of a boss are still seen, say the people.

In an editorial last week directed to the election of commissioners, Squire Dodd's name was inadvertently used where we meant Squire Leuty. We don't know which of them is entitled to our apology for the mistake.

Esquire J.L. Henry's friends say that he will discharge the chairman's duties in a fair, impartial manner. His first and best opportunity to prove this presents itself at once — notify the election commissioners of the vacancies in the court.

The Herald says that Rhea county would now have a high school but for the opposition of superintendent Rogers. Prof. Rogers is not in office now — not even a resident of the county.

Whose fault is it now that we are without a high school?

When county superintendent Rogers drew $400 salary per year The Herald thought it reckless extravagance.

When superintendent Frazier drew $600 a year, The Herald never cheaped. Now that the county court has practically increased his salary to $900 per year, what will this champion of economy say?   NIT

WANTED — Four men to canvass for the King Wagon Bed Hoister at $20 per week. Lift bed off and on easily. Retails at $4. Address J.J. King, inventor and patentee.   Athens, Tenn.

A SANTA CLAUS LETTER

The following labored epistle, written on a tear-stained, crumpled sheet, was found near the Herald office in Dayton, and is presumed to have miscarried:

Dear Santa Claus:

Please send me a real sympathetic friend, one who can make allowance for the alleged inconsistency of a Simon pure Democratic editor. I claim to be of the all-wool, -yard-wide, -true blue-regular-Wm. Jennings-anti-Cleveland-Chattanooga Times-variety, and to always support my party nominees except in the cases of Chancellor, County Representative, Sheriff and Trustee; and, because of these exceptions, they claim I am inconsistent. To bad, ain't it?

I claim to be conducting the "leading paper" in Rhea County, and to always stand for fair play, honesty and right, regardless of politics, except that in the last Register's race I published Denton as being elected when he was not, and when called on to make appropriate correction, declined to do so.

I insisted on the Election commissioners standing by the face of the returns in the case of Kelly, County Court Clerk, but declined to condemn them for going behind the face of the returns to elect Mr. Denton Register and J.L. Henry

Justice of the Peace. I claim to be consistent, however, and want a friend who can sympathize with me when charged with inconsistency.

As editor of the "leading paper" I read my rival's lectures on journalism, but never indulge in personalities, except in case of attorneys Swafford, Miller, Locke and a few others, and about this I am sorry.

An everlasting teetotaler, I have always been a consistent Prohibitionist, except in the case of M. Pattsfitrick [*sic*] and yet "they say" I am not consistent.

I am an advocate of Reform and Economy, especially in County affairs, except in case of the new Court which increased the salary of all its members, raised both their per diem and mileage, doubled the salary of County Superintendent, increased the salary of County Attorney, and made double as many unnecessary appropriations in one year as did the old Court, and, for this, my enemies say I am inconsistent.

Please send me one genuine sympathetic friend as I have none in this section, and I will hereafter be your good little boy.

Yours Truly, TOMMIE

THE county court of Anderson county doesn't seem to be composed altogether of mossbacks. A resolution to issue $100,000 in bonds for public roads passed Monday with a whoop, only a few of the sleepiest members daring to attempt to vote her down. Maybe Anderson signals an awakening in East Tennessee for a crusade against mud and moss-backs. — Chattanooga Press.

The greatest of all mountain railways is that which ascends Mt. Lowe, in southern California, to an altitude of 6,000 feet at a 48 per cent grade.

The New York Central railway carries 43 per cent of the freight which crosses the state of New York, while the Erie canal carries but 8 per cent.

ADVERTISEMENT FROM PAGE 6

ADVERTISEMENTS FROM PAGE 6

"HERMITAGE" FUND

It now seems probable, through the efforts of Hon. W.B. Miller, that Rhea county will come up with her pro rata for the reproduction of the "Hermitage" at St. Louis.

Mr. Miller got the county court to appropriate $170 toward the fund. This with other subscriptions he has secured gives assurance that Rhea will do her share toward the enterprise. Tennessee cannot afford to lose this opportunity of representation at the greatest fair on earth; Rhea can't afford to be behind her sister counties in the movemennt.

Advertised Letter List

Remaining in the Dayton Post Office uncalled for Jan. 2, 1904:

Ames, Mr. S.	Lagon, Mary
Boyd, J.A.	Mintan, L.E.
Colber, Emily	Mase, Mr. T.
Fragile, F.J.	McDresmant, Mrs. S.
Heath, Mrs. Tain	Parks, F.F.
Hughes, M.A.	Pool, W.T.B.
James, Mrs. Lizzie	Ridley, Rev. Lee
Jones, Miss Oda	Rathenberg, Mr. S.
Lane, Sarah	Rhymer, Mr. Sam
Lacy, Mr. E.	Snow, Mr. E.

JOHN MORGAN, POST MASTER

Students of ancient history are never up to date.

Temptation is the balance in which character is weighed.

Beware of the silent man; he may be a reformed prize fighter.

When a pessimist loses his mind it's a fortunate man who doesn't find it.

Some times a man can cure himself of insominia by trying to keep awake.

Many a man gets the best of a fish because he hasn't the nerve to run away.

When the young man in the parlor loses sight of the girl's mother he shouldn't forget the keyhole.

When a bachelor tells a married woman how happy he is she wouldn't be surprised to see him go the way of Ananias.

In London the schools are so crowded that sixty pupils per teacher is the average.

The peninsula of India which in area is half the size of the United States, has a population of 800,000,000, of whom 200,000,000 are farmers.

The telephone system of Uganda, in darkest Africa, is, with its branches, 1,084 miles in extent, the poles being living trees. The charge is 82 cents for each conversation over any distance.

Sir Richard Cartwright has given notice in the Canadian parliament of a resolution to make provision for a subsidy not exceeding $138,885 a year for a steamship service between Canada and France.

The per capita consumption of potatoes in the United States is three and three fourths bushels per annum, while in Germany it is twenty-eight and one fourth bushels. An acre in potatoes in Germany yields 200 bushels, in the United States ninety-six.

[Page 7]

Our Industrial Future
By OSCAR S. STRAUS

THE value of trade unions in raising the standard of living and in guarding the interests of labor, in regulating the hours and conditions of work, are benefits which organization has unquestionably promoted. The great hope of our industrial future is, that the working classes whose powers for good and for evil have been so strengthened by organization, will be guided by enlightened principles, and abstain from seeking proximate benefits in contravention of undoubted economic experiences and at the cost of fundamental rights. To the extent they misuse their great power, of arbitrary curtailing the rights of their fellow laborers or their employers, they array themselves against public sentiment, and from that day their power and their usefulness will decline. Even if labor organizations comprised the entire number of wageworkers in the country, this would give them no right either to override the personal liberty of those within or beyond their ranks, or to insist upon special prvileges or immunities. They must rely upon the justness of their cause, and to the extent that force is used, the boycott or the bludgeon, in compelling others to unite with them, to that extent they negative their own claim to being a brotherhood organization, whose purpose is to elevate and benefit the wage-earning class. But as a matter of fact, while labor organizations are very strong in some industries, they include only about 15 per cent of the wage earners of the country, and it must not be forgotten that organization, however powerful, can give no rights to curtail the personal liberty of the remaining 85 per cent of the wage earners of the country.

While the greatly increased organization of both laborers and employers is a fact which must be taken into consideration in discussing the industrial future, it must not be overlooked that however powerful these great interests may grow, they can only embrace a fraction of the people in any country. The general public is greater and many times more numerous than these two powerful bodies combined, and upon it must fall the heaviest losses that grow out of industrial war. The general public is patient, long-suffering and enduring. Its only organization is the general government, municipal, state and national, for the protection of the public welfare. Public opinion demands that the great public service corporations not only shall perform their function, but also they shall not be obstructed in that performance, and it also demands that the great avenues of supply and distribution of the necessities of life shall not be arbitrarily cut off in order to test the relative strength and enduring powers of the contending forces.

Organized labor and organized capital are in a fortunate state. They are both new to their acquired power. With time and experience a reaction in favor of conservatism will make itself felt, and in the meantime reconciliation will help rather than hinder a more reliable and permanent remedy.

Ingratitude of the Successful Man
By PROF. EDWARD AMHERST OTT

THERE is no lesson that we need to remind people of more in life than the lesson of gratitude to the means by which they rise. Some one has said that "ingratitude's a weed of every clime," and America certainly seems to provide soil in which the weed thrives and spreads.

The battle of life is not so easy and none of us fight it alone. The thoughts that we think are few of them ours. A friend suggests something that opens the doorway into a new life, but how often do we come back and tell him how he has helped us?

"Blow, blow, thou winter wind.
Thou art not so unkind
        As man's ingratitude;
Thy tooth is not so keen,
Because thou art not seen,
        Although thy breath be rude."
                                — Shakespear

I wish that our great men would remember their beginnings better. Our rich men, in the time of their prosperity, forget all the bright, sweet things that in the days of their hopes and struggles they had vowed to do. They leave the place where they gained their wealth, the place of their beginnings.

Evolution of Ethics
By DR. EMIL G. HIRSCH

MEN of future generations will regard with horror and surprise the morals of the world of to-day. The present generation stands aghast at the thought that civilized men should hold their fellow beings in slavery, and the men of future generations will view with equal horror our belief that it is proper to build up large fortunes at the expense of character. They will wonder how it was that at the beginning of the twentieth century enlightened men in France, Germany and Russia could be prejudiced against other men because they were born of Jewish parents. They will wonder why it was that the men of to-day believed that it was right and proper to steal money from the government, and thought it wrong only to be caught at it.

Ethics are subject to the law of evolution, even as are life and education and religion. The doctrine of evolution is not opposed to religion, but those who understand the basic truths upon which all religions are founded appreciate the fact that religion itself was built up by a process of evolution. This doctrine is as old as the chapter in the book of Genesis which declared that Noah was "a righteous man in his generation," the phrase, "in his generation," meaning that Noah might not have been considered either religious or moral according to the standards of the generations that followed.

If you don't try to live up to your ideals the chances are they'll come down — Puck.

Selfishness is always shortsighted. — Ram's Horn.

Wild oats make worse bread. — Ram's Horn.

Life without toil would be without triumph. — Chicago Journal.

A happy disposition is merely a disposition to make others happy. — Puck.

ADVERTISEMENTS FROM PAGE 7

ADVERTISEMENTS FROM PAGE 7

Nature's Greatest Cure for Men and Women

Swamp-Root is the Most Perfect Healer and Natural Aid to the Kidneys, Liver and Bladder Ever Discovered.

"Swamp-Root Saved My Life."

A FARMER'S STRONG TESTIMONIAL.

I received promptly the sample bottle of your kidney remedy, Swamp-Root.

I had an awful pain in my back, over the kid-

MR. T. S. APKER.

neys, and had to urinate from four to seven times a night, often with smarting and burning. Brick dust would settle in the urine. I lost twenty pounds in two weeks and thought I would soon die. I took the first dose of your Swamp-Root in the evening at bed time, and was very much surprised; I had to urinate but once that night, and the second night I did not get up until morning. I have used three bottles of Swamp-Root and to-day am as well as ever.

I am a farmer and am working every day, and weigh 190 pounds, the same that I weighed before I was taken sick.

Gratefully yours,

Sec. F. A. & I. U. 504.   T. S. APKER,
April 9th, 1903.   Marsh Hill, Pa.

There comes a time to both men and women when sickness and poor health bring anxiety and trouble hard to bear; disappointment seems to follow every effort of physicians in our behalf, and remedies we try have little or no effect. In many such cases serious mistakes are made in doctoring, and not knowing what the disease is or what makes us sick. Kind nature warns us by certain symptoms, which are unmistakable evidence of danger, such as too frequent desire to urinate, scanty supply, scalding irritation, pain or dull ache in the back —they tell us in silence that our kidneys need doctoring. If neglected now, the disease advances until the face looks pale or sallow, puffy or dark circles under the eyes, feet swell, and sometimes the heart acts badly.

There is comfort in knowing that Dr. Kilmer's Swamp-Root, the great kidney, liver and bladder remedy, fulfills every wish in quickly relieving such troubles. It corrects inability to hold urine and scalding pain in passing it, and overcomes that unpleasant necessity of being compelled to get up many times during the night to urinate. In taking this wonderful new discovery Swamp-Root you afford natural help to nature, for Swamp-Root is the most perfect helper and gentle aid to the kidneys that has ever been discovered.

Swamp-Root a Blessing to Women.

My kidneys and bladder gave me great trouble for over two months and I suffered untold misery.

MRS. E. AUSTIN.

I became weak, emaciated and very much run down. I had great difficulty in retaining my urine, and was obliged to pass water very often night and day. After I had used a sample bottle of Dr. Kilmer's Swamp-Root, sent me on my request; I experienced relief and I immediately bought of my druggist two large bottles and continued taking it regularly. I am pleased to say that Swamp-Root cured me entirely. I can now stand on my feet all day without any bad symptoms whatever. Swamp-Root has proved a blessing to me.   Gratefully yours,

Mrs. E. Austin,
19 Nassau St., Brooklyn, N. Y.

To Prove What SWAMP-ROOT, the Great Kidney, Liver and Bladder Remedy Will do for YOU, Every Reader of Our Paper May Have a Sample Bottle FREE by Mail.

ADVERTISEMENTS FROM PAGE 7

Curses come home to roost and blessings come home to rest. — Ram's Horn.

Be loyal, and if you can't, at least put up a decent bluff. — Chicago Tribune.

If you don't want to borrow anything, everbody has something to lend. — Casswells.

He — "Tell you what. Let's found a society for mutual admiration. I, for instance, admire your beautiful eyes, and what do you admire in me?"

She— "Your good taste."— New Yorker.

Willie — "Pa, when you say a man's 'wool gathering,' it means he's lazy, don't it?"

Pa — "Not necessarily. He may be gathering the wool off the lambs in Wall street," — Philadelphia Ledger.

Injustice — Mr. Richfello — "What a peachy complexion Miss Beauti has!"

Rival Belle — "You do her injustice, really, Mr. Richfello. Her face isn't so very fuzzy — except on her upper lip." — New York Weekly.

Unconditional — "You can't bring about the universal brotherhood of man by legal enactment." "Why not?" "Why not? Well, for one thing, the universal brotherhood of man would be in derogation of vested rights," — Detroit Free Press.

Not a Repeater — "These old proverbs make me weary," sighed the professor. "What's the matter now?" queried the other half of the sketch. "Here's one that says 'History repeats itself,' " replied the learned person, "and any schoolboy knows that isn't true." — Chicago Daily News.

Tess — "He proposed to me to-day, and he was so impatient. He wanted me to marry him right away. But I was not to be hurried."

Jess — "So you put him off, eh?"

Tess — "Yes, indeed. I told him he'd have to wait until tomorrow." — Philadelphia Press.

"Yes, he fooled me completely. He had such a smooth way with him."

"Which proves that the way of the transgressor is most successful when it's smooth." — Philadelphia Ledger.

Sportsman (wishing for fresh fields to conquer) — "I should like to try my hand at big game."

Fair Ignoramus — "Yes, I suppose you find it very hard to hit these little birds!" — Punch.

Trying to Stump the Professor

Smarte — You see me queer the professor. I'll make him own up there's one thing at least he doesn't know.

Smarte (to professor) — Will you please tell me, Mr. Wyse, who was Cain's wife?

"Cain's wife, Mr. Smarte, was Adam's daughter-in-law."— Boston Transcript.

ADVERTISEMENTS FROM PAGE 8

ADVERTISEMENTS FROM PAGE 8

(Page 8)

TENNESSEE NEWS
TERSELY TOLD

Friends of Judge Smallman of Warren county, claims that he will come out for congress against Judge John A. Moon of the third district.

T.B. Johnson, attorney for the state in the Womack saloon cases, decided in Franklin, stated that the cases would be appealed to the supreme court.

W.L. Meers of a St. Louis contracting firm has arrived in Knoxville and is making preparations to begin work on the new passenger station in that city.

Gov. Frazier has refused to pardon J.L. Wallace of Blount county sentenced to three years in the penitentiary for killing a young man named Campbell at Maryville.

The trials of Jim Shoemaker, Dennis Graves and Earl Formstom, charged with hold-ups in Knoxville, resulted in each being bound over in $10,000 and in default were sent to jail.

John Carlow and John Sparks have been arrested by a United States deputy marshal at La-Follette on the charge of counterfeiting. They were taken to Knoxville and committed to jail by Commissioner Carter.

Produce Market

Corrected weekly by N.D. Reed & Sons.
Chicken Hens — 20c - 25c;   Fryers 12c - 20c.
Beeswax — 22c - 25c.
Ginseng — $4.00 - $4.50.
Eggs — 23c.   Butter — 20c.
Irish Potatoes — 60c. Onions — 75c.
Wheat — 80 - 90c.   Peas — $1.00.
Corn — 50c.   Feathers — 25 - 50c.
No. 1 hay — $15.00 per ton.
Dry hides — 10 - 12½c.
Furs — coons 25c to 75c; o'possum 10c to 50c;
   muskrats 5c to 20c; skunks 10c to $1.00;
   otter $3.00 to $10.00; Beaver $3.00 to
   $7.00; Fox 50c to $1.50.

R-I-P-A-N-S Tabules. Doctors find a good prescription for mankind. The 5¢ package is enough for any usual occasion. The family bottle (60¢) contains a supply for a year. All druggists.

ADVERTISEMENTS FROM PAGE 8

20 PER CNT DISCOUNT SALE.

Beginning Dec. 15th and lasting 30 days only, now if yOu miss this Very, Very rare op oportunity you will feel like killing yourself when you see such Bargains as yuor neighbor s have made at WALLINGFORD'S 20 per cen t Discount sale.

It matters not with You whether I am Going OUT of Businss. or Going INTO Business. What You want is the following

PRICES:

More Shoes And Better Than any one House in he a County. Punchouts City and County Warrants taken At 80ȼ On The Dollar In This Sale. School Warrants 08ȼ. Men, Ladies And Boys ain Cont 10ȼ on the Dollar Thus $0.00 cent cost you 8.00 150 cost you 75ȼ They must go.	Prices $5 00 Shoe for $4 00 " $4 00 Shoe for $3 20 " $3 50 Shoe for $2 80 " $3 00 Shoe for $2 40 " $2 50 Shoe for 2 00 " 2 25 Shoe for 1 80 " 2 00 Shoe for 1 60 " 1 75 Shoe for 1 40 " 1-50 Shoe for 1 20 " 1 25 Shoe fcr 1 00 " 1 00 Shoe for 80 " 90 Shoe for 72 " 80 Shoe for 64 " 75 Shoe for 60 " 60 Shoe for 48 " 50 Shoe for 40 " 25 shoe for 20	I am determined to Have an Exclusive Shoe house in Dayton This is for cash only no goods Charged At These Prices. Any One Trying to Jew us below these prices will be considered on the charity list and we will treat them accordingly

Boys, what better present do you want for sweetheart than a nice pair of bed-room slippers? Sweethearts, what do you think would please your brother or somebody else's brother better than a nice pair of house slippers, gloves or ties, which you can get at WALLINGFORD'S. $2.00 worth of anything you want cost $1.60 $1.00 worth of anything you want cost 80 cents Dont miss this chance, all goods marked in plain figures and it will cost you nothing to look.

J. G. WALLINGFORD.

THE WEEKLY HERALD

A HERALD OF BETTER THINGS—ALWAYS PROGRESSIVE

1898 SIXTH ANNIVERSARY 1904

DAYTON. TENN.

FRIDAY JUNE 24 1904

PLANT OF DAYTON MILLING CO.

LAUREL FALLS NEAR DAYTON

IT IS THE CENTER AND PRINCIPAL SHIPPING POINT OF THE GREAT STRAWBERRY & FRUIT BELT OF EAST TENNESSEE

BIRDS-EYE VIEW OF DAYTON FROM HILL CITY SCHOOL BUILDING.

SURROUNDED BY COAL, IRON, LIMESTONE & TIMBER TEMPERATE & HEALTHFUL CLIMATE PURE AIR, CLEAR COLD WATER AND FREE HAPPY PEOPLE

THE CITY OF DAYTON WITH ITS SUBURBS CONTAINS A POPULATION OF 3500 PEOPLE AND IS THE POLITICAL INDUSTRIAL AND COMMERCIAL METROPOLIS OF RHEA COUNTY.

A RHEA COUNTY BERRY FARM

VOL. VII NO. I 50¢ PER YEAR

FURNACE OF DAYTON COAL & IRON CO.

PAGE 1 OF ANNIVERSARY ISSUE

THE WEEKLY HERALD
[24 JUNE 1904]

This special edition of *The Weekly Herald* contained a total of 16 pages. The outside sheet of four pages was made up of full-page advertisements. These are reproduced on pages 27, 28, 71, and 72.

THE WEEKLY HERALD.

Issued Every Friday.

T. J. CAMPBELL, Ed. and Bus. Mgr.
CLAUDE R. GIVENS, City Editor.

OFFICE: Hudson Block, Up-Stairs

Entered at the Post Office at Dayton, Tennessee, as second-class matter for transmission through the mails.

SUBSCRIPTION RATES.

One Year (in advance) 50c
Six Months 30c
Three Months 20c

A rate of 75c will be charged when not paid in advance.

A simple X mark opposite your name indicates that your subscription has expired while a XX shows you are in arrears.

[Page 3]

RHEA COUNTY OFFICIALS

The following pen and pencil sketches of those who manage the business affairs of our county will be of interest to many:

Chairman J. L. HENRY

J L HENRY

J. L. Henry, justice of the peace and present chairman of the county court, was born on Yellow Creek in Rhea county (on what is now the Chattin place) on the 31 day of December, 1844, and is now in his sixtieth year.

He was raised on a farm and received only such educational advantages as the country schools of those days afforded.

When a mere boy in 1863 he joined Capt. W.S. Greer's company in the 1st Tennessee Cav., commanded by Col. Jas. E. Carter, and served until the close of the war. He saw service in the celebrated Valley compaign in Virginia in 1864, at the seige of Knoxville with Longstreet and also in Tennessee and Kentucky.

He was married in 1873 to Mary J. Rudd, daughter of E.L. Rudd, of this county. They have five children, four boys and a girl.

In 1876 he was elected justice of the peace and with the exception of one term of six years has filled the office almost continuously since, this making his second term as chairman of the county court. In politics he is a consistent democrat and in religion a Baptist.

His life, with the exception of four years, has been spent in Rhea county and he is generally known throughout the county. His residence is Dayton.

W.B. KELLY, County Court Clerk

W.B. Kelly, the present popular clerk of the county court, is a native of Rhea county having been born on a farm near Washington some forty-three years ago. Most of his life has been spent on the farm, though he has filled several positions in the commercial world, one of them being with the Dayton Coal & Iron Co.

W B KELLY

Though always an ardent democrat, Mr. Kelly never held or sought public office until he was nominated and elected to the office he now holds in the August election, 1902. In that election according to the vote as conducted by the precinct officers, Mr. Kelly was given a majority of 89, but between the closing of the polls Thursday evening and the following Monday, when the vote was recounted by the commissioners of election, many changes were surreptitiously made in the ballots so that the recount showed a majority of 65 for his opponent, Mr. C.L. Hayes, who was given a certificate of election and inducted into office. Mr. Kelly at once contested the election and after one of the bitterest fights known in the courts of Rhea county and the state lasting some fifteen months he was awarded the office to which the people had elected him.

The subject of this sketch was married in 1883 to Miss Ada Morrison, of Dycusville, Ky., and they have two sons, the fruit of this marriage. Mr. Kelly is a member of the Cumberland Presbyterian church, but is quite liberal in his contributions to other churches.

W. B. ALLEN, Circuit Court Clerk

W.B. Allen was born at Decatur, Tenn., June 5, 1869, and was educated in the high school at that place. He came to Dayton in September, 1886, and has resided here ever since. Soon after coming here he entered the Dayton City Bank as Teller, was elected Cashier in April in 1889 and remained Cashier of the Dayton City Bank and the First National Bank of Dayton for about five years.

W B ALLEN

Later he accepted a position as book-keeper with Dayton Coal & Iron Company, where he was employed when appointed Circuit Court Clerk by Judge Smallman in October 1899, to fill the vacancy caused by the death of Charles G. Gillespie. He was nominated by the democratic convention to succeed himself in the spring of 1900 and was elected in August following; he was renominated and re-elected for the full term of four years without opposition in 1902.

Mr. Allen is a member of the M.E. Church South and has been a steward almost continuously for the past fifteen years, and has several times been elected a delegate to the annual conference.

He is a Knight of Pythias and has twice been Chancellor Commander of Hope Lodge No. 27 and now holds the position of deputy Grand Chancellor.

As clerk of the court Mr. Allen is pronounced the best on his circuit. He is efficient, curteous and accomodating. As a candidate he is a democrat, but as an official he is a gentleman who knows no party, sect, creed or condition in the discharge of his duty.

N. J. TALLENT, Sheriff

N.J. Tallent, the present high sheriff of Rhea county, was born in Marshall county, Ala., Feb. 5, 1873, but removed with his parents to Rhea county when only two years of age, where he has since resided.

Being the oldest son of a somewhat numerous family of children he, at an early age, became the chief support of a widowed mother, and learned by experience how to meet and overcome the most serious problems of life.

N J TALLENT

From his early childhood he was serious, sober, honest and industrious, and laid the foundations for the splendid business success that he achieved in his youthful manhood.

He has been a resident of Dayton from his childhood and has been closely identified with the growth of the town.

For a number of years he engaged successfully in the livery business, has served the city as marshal, and for the past two years has filled the office of high sheriff of the county in a manner highly creditable to himself.

In every relation of life he has applied strict principles of business integrity, and he enjoys in a high degree the confidence and good will of the public.

Mr. Tallent has recently been renominated by the republicans of the county for re-election to the office of sheriff, and regardless of what the result may be, the public generally understand that his canvass will be clean and honest, for Noah Tallent is a clean, honest, honorable gentleman.

J. W. VANCE, Trustee

Mr. John W. Vance, the present popular incumbent of the office of Trustee of Rhea county, is a native of Pennsylvania, where he resided until about the year 1884 when he removed to Alabama.

After a residence of six years in Alabama, he accepted employment under the Dayton Coal & Iron Co. as superintendent of the coke ovens, which position he filled to the entire satisfaction of his employees for about fifteen years.

Mr. Vance is an elder in the Presbyterian church, and has held the responsible office of Master of Finance in the K. of P. Lodge for the past ten years — he having been elected to this office without opposition, at each annual election since 1898.

J W VANCE

He was elected to the office of Trustee in 1902 and is therefore serving his first term. His administration of the affairs of the office has been creditable to himself and satisfactory to the public.

In politics, Mr. Vance is a republican and has been again nominated by his party for the office of Trustee.

ADVERTISEMENT FROM PAGE 3

ADVERTISEMENTS FROM PAGE 3

[Page 4]

The Records of Rhea County
A Historical Sketch

----o----

(Written for THE HERALD by Col. W.L. GIVENS)

Only fragmentary parts of the public records of Rhea county for the first fifteen years of its existence as a county have been preserved, these records having been carelessly destroyed in time of the war, while the old court house at Washington was being used as a military post and as headquarters for the U.S. Provost Marshal.

The early records of the county, however, are very strange and interesting to students of history, containing as they do the only account of many events of vital importance to the growth and prosperity of the county.

From the year 1796, when the state of Tennessee was admitted into the union, up to the year 1801, the territory now comprising Rhea county was a part of Knox county, designated as the Hamilton District, and known as Cumberland Valley. In 1804, Roane county was established and Rhea was a part of Roane county until the year 1807 when by Chapter 9 of the Acts of the General Assembly, Rhea county was established.

The act creating the county appointed five commissioners, who were authorized to select a suitable site for the seat of justice, and for the county town, to procure by purchase or otherwise fifty acres of land therefor.

These commissioners were to name the town, execute a deed to the lands bought by them as commissioners, which commissioners were authorized to divide the land secured for a town site into town lots, advertise and sell the same, and superintend the erection of a court-house and jail.

The following named parties were appointed by the county court as comissioners, to-wit: T.J.[sic] Campbell, David Murphree, Robt. Patterson, John Roddye and Daniel Walker. [NOTE: Givens has omitted some names and combined the appointments from two years. The correct list from 1809 is: Jesse Roddye, Alexander Ferguson, Azariah David, Daniel Rawlings, Robert Patterson, and David Campbell. The 1811 commissioners were James Campbell, Jesse Roddye, Alexander Ferguson, Azariah David, Daniel Rawlings, David Murphree, Daniel Walker, and John Locke. B.J.B.]

These commissioners appear to have served the county for six years at least, and they may have served longer as the records containing their final report have been destroyed.

Many town lots were conveyed by them up to the year 1818, ranging in price from $6.00 to $15.00 per lot, according to location.

In 1821 the legislature passed an act extending the lines of Rhea county across the Tennessee river so as to embrace the territory now in Meigs county, known as a part of the "Hiwassee District" which territory was at once surveyed by the surveyor general and divided into townships and sections.

This was the only part of Rhea county that was ever surveyed and divided into townships by state authority, for the reason that all of the land in the county, east of the foot of the mountain, had been taken up by two grants, one for nineteen thousand acres, the other for twenty thousand acres issued by the state of North Carolina to Stokely Donaldson in 1775.

From the organization of the county in 1807 until the year 1834, the county was divided into militia districts or divisions, with each division under a captain, and the property in these districts was listed for taxation, as "taxable in Captain 'A's' Company" etc., and then followed a list of the names of all the land owners within said militia division, with the number of acres of land owned by each.

In 1822 there were nine militia divisions in Rhea county commanded by nine captains. In this year the total number of acres of land listed for taxation was 66,466. The basis of taxation was one hundred acres of land regardless of location or value.

In 1822, the total levy on each one hundred acres of land in Rhea county was 81¼ cents, divided as follows:

State tax	18 ¾
County	43 ¾
Pauper	18 ¾

In this year the total taxation on each town lot in the county regardless of location, character or value of the improvement thereon was $1.56¼. There were 49 town lots listed for this year, 458 free polls and 127 black polls. The total revenue for the county for the year 1822 derived from all sources was $941.96¾.

In 1845, an act passed levying a tax of $5.00 on all four wheeled vehicles kept for pleasure; and it is a curious fact that for eight years thereafter when the act was repealed there was only one such vehicle reported each year.

The records do not show to whom this vehicle belonged, but the presumption is that it is the same high wheeled buggy now used by Captain Ace Templeton in his daily trips to and from Dayton.

In 1835 [1836] Meigs county was established and the Tennessee river was again made the boundary line of Rhea county. By this act Rhea county lost fully one-half its population, and according to the amount of land listed for taxation she lost 72,014½ acres of land cut off to Meigs county.

In this division all the larger and more important lands on the Tennessee river were given to Meigs county, thus giving to that county a total frontage of 173 miles.

The good old county of Rhea is rich in legends and traditions that are fast fading from the memory of men.

Many of her sons have distinguished themselves in various callings, but their deeds are only preserved by tradition and in a few years their names even will have been forgotten among men.

How many of the present inhabitants of Rhea county have ever heard of Judge Campbell, the able jurist, the eloquent advocate, the just judge, who was among the first, if not the very first of Rhea county's lawyers? How many have heard of the excentric Dr. John Hoyle, the blacksmith doctor, who ranked high in his profession and accumulated a handsome fortune? Although it is said of him that he never refused to attend a charity patient.

How many have heard of the Rev. R. Tate Howard? Just a few years dead, yet in his day one of the most earnest, powerful and eloquent evangelists that the state ever produced, and one who would rank with the foremost evangelists of any country.

A history of Rhea county, with personal reminiscences and biographical sketches of some of her pioneer citizens would read like a romance.

"Old Washington"

---o---

(By Hon. V. C. ALLEN)

Rhea county was created by Chapter 9 Acts of 1897 of the Legislature of Tennessee. After the organization of the county in 1808 the officials met at the house of Wm. Henry, who resided in the valley north of Dayton and near the Kyle residence. Here the first court was held and commissioners were appointed to locate the county seat for the new county.

These commissioners were anxious to locate the capital of Rhea on the Tennessee river, and went, by their official report shows, to "Hazel Riggs" [Haslerig's] shoals, where Tom F. Robinson now lives, and had about agreed to locate the town there. On their return trip in crossing back water, Commissioner Handy was drowned near what has been known since as "Handy's Pond" on the road leading from the Robinson place to Washington. This accident changed the location to Washington. The records fail to show whether the town was named for George Washington of "cherry tree" fame or for "Billy" Washington, the "Hatter," who lived at that time on the hill in

a cabin near what was formerly known as the "old Murphy place" afterward where Col. J.W. Gillespie resided [NOTE: the town was named before the site was chosen. B.J.B.]. Miller Frances, the grandfather of Governor Peter Turney and the first sheriff of Rhea county, erected and occupied a small house near where C.L. Locke's residence now stands.

The first court was held in Washington in 1810 [1812] in a log house that stood where Locke's store house now stands. A frame structure succeeded this, and was situated on the hill near where the brick temple of justice was erected by Crutchfield (the father of Wm. and Tom Crutchfield of Chattanooga) which was standing and in use for a court house when the county seat was removed to Dayton.

After the Hiwassee purchase in 1819, the limits of Rhea county were extended and included all of what is now Meigs county. Soon after this, Washington became a prosperous town and in 1830 had quite a number of good business houses, boasting at that time of two wholesale houses and was defeated for the state capital by only one vote [no proof of this. B.J.B.]

Washington then had four hotels or "taverns" as they were then called. The Liberty Hotel, Freeman, Kennedy & Parker and Homes. Among the oldest merchants were Gillespie & Co., the Inmans, Waterhouse, McCallie & Hook, John D. Traynor and others. John [Franklin] Locke, J.C. Mitchell, T.J. Campbell were the leading lawyers. The town also had two cotton gins, a large tannery and other industries. A newspaper called "The Valley Freeman" run by the Messers. Hood was published then.

Judge Campbell, the first chairman of the county court after Washington became the capital of Rhea, built a house northeast of the cemetery and died there, but was buried near "Town Creek" in what was known as the R.N. Gillespie meadow.

A large brick church was erected north of courthouse hill which was blown down about 1850. Afterwards a large hewed log church was erected near the cemetery, called Monmouth church, then followed the frame building on the hill south of the old court house.

When Ross' Landing (Chattanooga) began to attract attention as to the Gateway to the South, some of the best business men left Washington for that point; business houses were torn down and the brick taken to Chattanooga in flat boats. The old house on hill east of town, on J.G. and Walter Tomison's farm, where James Carney now lives, was erected by John Locke, and a branch of the State bank of Tennessee was once located in that building.

In 1836 Meigs county was created. This took about one-half of Rhea county's territory and a number of her most progressive citizens, but Old Washington still remained a good country town. At the beginning of the civil war she had some wealthy and substantial business men; such men as R.N. Gillespie, Joseph Parks, W.E. Colville, W.P. Darwin, Onslow Bean, F.J. Paine and others.

The writer was a school boy, but he well remembers the strength of Old Washington's citizenship in 1861. Prof. Martin White was teaching in the old brick academy on the hill west of Dr. Hoyal's residence, and the town and ---?--- [hole in newspaper] was noted for intelligence, ---?--- and refinement. But alas, redhanded war swept the anti-bellum hospitality from the South.

Washington suffered in common with other southern towns. Property was swept away, houses burned, and the greatest loss still was in her brave, manly men who fell in the deadly conflict. After the war came the C.S. railway and then the removal of the county seat, leaving but a memory of Old Washington.

ADVERTISEMENT FROM PAGE 4

ADVERTISEMENTS FROM PAGE 4

Reminiscences

---o---

(Written for THE HERALD by H.A. CRAWFORD)

Many changes have taken place in the Old Volunteer State since the birth of Russell Bean, the first white child born in the territory now forming the state. Russell's father, William Bean, was the first permanent white settler, and built the log cabin on the banks by the historic Watauga river in 1769 in which his son was born.

The Watauga Association vested governmental powers in five commissioners in 1772, viz: John Sevier, James Robertson, Charles Robertson, Zachariah Isbell and John Carter, selected a sheriff, clerk and other officers and constituted the first purely republican free and independent government established and administered in the northern Hemisphere.

In 1780, the first school and the first church in what is now the state was established by Samuel Doak near Jonesboro in Washington county. The school became Washington College and was the first literary institution established in the Mississippi Valley. The church was and is now old Salem Presbyterian Church.

In February, 1795, delegates chosen by the people from eleven counties, being at that time all the counties organized in the territory, met at Knoxville and adopted a state constitution and on the suggestion of Andrew Jackson (Old Hickory), one of the delegates, selected and gave the new state the name of "Tennessee." The first session of the first General Assembly of the state opened at Knoxville on March 28, 1796; June 1, 1796, Tennessee was admitted by congress into the union of states.

Much of the foregoing is a matter of history which the school boys and girls know, or can know, by consulting the school histories of the state.

Some of the delegates from the eleven counties represented in the constitutional convention are probably ancestors of citizens of Rhea county. Among the number such familiar names appear as Samuel Frazier, James Roddye, Spencer Clack, John Clack, Elisha Baker, John Galbreath, James Berry, John Rhea, John Crawford and others.

Almost a century has passed since Rhea county took her place as one of the counties of the state — in 1807 it became a county. Meigs county until 1835 formed a part of Rhea.

The first seat of justice in Rhea was at William Henrys, called later Big Spring, now the David Kyle place in the valley four miles above Dayton. The temple of justice was a large hewed log structure and near it another building was erected of like material in which was placed vile law-breakers of that time. The courts were held at this place until probably 1812 or 1813 when Washington became the county sat. Miller Francis was the first sheriff of the county, Daniel Rawlings first county court clerk. They each served in their respective offices many years and probably until 1820.

Judge N.Q. Allen says in his interesting sketch of the sheriffs of the country, written for the Dayton Leader several years ago, that "prior to 1820 no authentic records of the county court can be found, but that Miller Francis commenced acting as sheriff not later than 1809 and served continuously until 1820 when he was succeeded by his brother, Woodson Francis. Miller Francis was grand-father, on his mother's side, of Tennessee's able and venerable governor Peter Turney." Doubtless Judge Allen is correct in this matter. The writer knows that his friend Nick spent considerable time in getting up reliable data for his admirable sketch. After 1820, we have authentic records of the courts which any one interested can examine when they desire to do so.

Through the courtesy of Miss Alice Waterhouse, of Washington, the writer has been permitted to examine a very complete and interesting diary kept by her grandfather, Richard Green

Waterhouse, through a time of perhaps ninety years. Mr. Waterhouse when quite a young man left his father's home in New Jersey and by easy stages made his way to Knoxville, arriving there early in 1800. He lived for a time in Iredell on the opposite side of the river from Knoxville and operated a ferry there. In December 1809, he removed in flat boats to a place he had previously bought in Tennessee Valley, near Piney river in Rhea county. He was a man of much intelligence and energy and accumulated a large amount of property, owning at one time 100,000 acres of land, situated principally in East Tennessee.

From the diary mentioned, it appears that he attended the Rhea county courts from 1808 to 1812 at William Henry's home, as before mentioned, and transacted business with Miller Francis, sheriff, and Daniel Rawlings, clerk. About Christmas, 1809, he was at the house of Little Page Sims, who then lived on Muddy Creek in Rhea county, where he met John Sevier, governor of the state, his wife and daughter, Betsy, who had come there on a visit.

Circuit court commenced operations in Rhea county March, 1810; first term ever held in the county. On March 23, 1810, went with commissioners and others to view a site for county town across the mouth of Richland — not approved. David Campbell made a deed to the commissioners of the town of Washington for 47 acres of land at the head of Spring Creek on the 27 of June, 1812.

In June 1812, Waterhouse made deeds to Letitia Vandyke and others for lots in Southern Liberties (Southern Liberties was a suburb of Washington, just south of town and was laid off into building lots and streets and at an early date contained several houses. The Letitia Vandyke mentioned was probably a relative of the Chancellor T. Nixon Vandyke. The judge was born in Washington).

Before Meigs county was taken from Rhea it is said Washington contained ten stores, three taverns or hotels, a branch of the State Bank, a newspaper — "The Valley Freeman" —

several blacksmiths and cabinet maker's shops, a turner's, and saddlery and harness shops, a tannery and three large cotton gins. Cotton was at that time one of the staple products of the country. Cottonport, on the river, was so named from the large amount of the staple shipped from that point. In the memory of the writer a large cotton warehouse stood on the bank of the river at that place.

The coming of the steamer Cherokee from the river to Washington on the high water of 1867 is of a more recent date than most matters to which this imperfect sketch is pertinent, but that occurrence is remembered by many citizens. But that a flat boat came out from the river on the backwater probably sometime in the thirties and was loaded with cotton at the Washington spring and was poled or rowed back to the river is an occurence not generally known. There can be but little doubt as to the correctness of this statement if we are to believe citizens who were at that time residents of the town.

There were no steamboats on the upper Tennessee until the little sidewheel sreamer Atlas came over the Muscle Shoals in 1829. After that date came at longer and shorter intervals the Enterprise, Knoxville, Guide, Harkaway, Reliance, first Holston, Cassandra, Huntsman, and Athens. The Huntsman came up about 1843 or 1844. Sometime in the forties a Mr. Dickson, who was cook on the Huntsman, killed a Mr. Clingam, an employee on the boat, at Washington landing. Dickson was placed in the Washington jail— true bill for murder was found by the grand jury. His trial was continued from court to court for several years on account of failure to procure witnesses. Finally, some of the witnesses died, others left the state,

ADVERTISEMENT FROM PAGE 5

and Dickson was released from prison after being incarcerated about six years.

Before the days of steamboating on the Tennessee river, merchants hauled their goods and wares from Baltimore. Four and six horse wagons of large capacity were used and it required nearly a month to make the trip. Freight rates were necessarily very high and with freight added to the high prices of nearly all manufactured articles, most people had to be content with a much smaller quantity of such things than now. A large part of all wearing appearel was made at home.

Below is a copy of one of the notes for borrowed money made to agent of the State Bank, John Locke, Esq., at Washington:

$116.00

One hundred and eighty days after date, we promise to pay William C. Mynatt, Agent for the Branch Bank of the State of Tennessee at Knoxville, or order one hundred and sixteen dollars at the Agency of Rhea county, for value received. Witness our hands and seals, the 29th November 1834.   J. D. TRAYNOR,   L.S.
T. N. GILLESPIE,   L.S.
ANSON DEARMON, L.S.
Attest, RICHARD WATERHOUSE."

Washingtom was once a prosperous little town with an excellent citizenship and good schools, a bright prospect was before her, but by a combination of unfavorable circumstances she has grown smaller by degrees and distressingly less. The division of the county gave her the first back-set, then the railroad gave her the"go by" and the removal of the county seat from her was the last straw that broke the camel's back. Many of her citizens have gone to other places, some have become citizens of and have contributed to the building up of Chattanooga, Cleveland, Dalton, Ga., Dayton and other places and many rest in peace in her environs. There are still some excellent citizens living in the old town and vicinity who are yet holding the fort.

ADVERTISEMENTS FROM PAGE 5

[Page 6]

The Parent and The School
(By SUPT. F. B. FRAZIER)

The work of the teacher is certainly a noble work. It ought to be a great deal more pleasant and agreeable. Especially is this true when we consider the causes which hamper the work of the profession and which curtail its desirable results. The good teacher could not ask for more praise than is already bestowed upon her; her honor is certainly unimpeached and her service to the country is recognized as invaluable and indispensible. Of these she does not need more. But there is one thing that would lighten her troubles and make many a dark day bright and that is the real heart felt sympathy of the parents — the fathers and mothers of the community.

The teacher has many difficulties to overcome, many obstacles to surmount, the which I shall not endeavor to enumerate. For my purpose it is enough to note that most of these difficulties arise from lack of sympathy and cooperation on the part of the parents. Many times when a teacher goes into a strange community we see the parents, or least some of them, looking for defects in the teacher instead of good qualities. The child is always ready to report the actions of a teacher to the ears of their parents, leaving off something here and adding something there until a clear case of partiality or favoritism is made out against the teacher. Many times the teacher is tried and publicly condemned by testimony carried by a "young blood" who has possibly been most justly "lashed."

Then, too much is often excepted of a teacher in school government. Some parents are inclined to compare the government of the school with that of the home. No greater mistake could be made than this. Besides controlling possibly fifty characters the teacher must continually conduct important recitations. The child has no appeal from the home government, but he is often encouraged to make the home an appeal court from the school wherein he is encouraged and instructed to present the appeals from the personally disagreeable conduct of his teacher.

Again misunderstandings often arise from a disposition on the part of some to want to dictate to the teacher. When a new teacher comes into a community she will invariably find some parents who, without particular investigation, have decided that their children should leave off this study and take up that one, eager to tell just how the school should be run and all about every body in particular. Such people are perfectly ready to take the opinions and medicine of their doctors without a word of dissent, but they usually feel that they can advise the teacher to advantage.

Many times the parents condemn a teacher because she does not teach like they were taught years ago. They are adverse to the use of modern apparatus in the school room and to buying many books and the like just because such things were not used when they went to school. Method, devices and apparatus are continually changing and the verdict of educators is that it is for the better. Therefore, the up-to-date teacher must keep in line and to do so must have proper tools to work with. The parent should be ever ready to leave the teacher the judge in all such matters and should cheerfully furnish anything suggested by the teacher provided it is possible for him to do so.

But of all these defects possibly the greatest is the irregular attendance of the pupils. Possibly nothing hinders the efficiency of the schools so much as this. It deranges and disorganizes the school and doubtless in many cases the work of the teacher. A child who is in school only about half of the time had better to all intents and purposes not be in school at all. A day missed causes the next day to be almost a failure because the student is behind. Then a few more days out will result in discouragement and finally in withdrawal on some slight pretext. Irregular attendance not only hinders the efficient working of the school but it makes much more difficult the work of the teacher as well and hinders the steady progress of the school. It is wonderful to note the petty excuses offered for a day's absence causing injuries to the child not to be counted in dollars and cents. The child is often kept from a school a day in order to go to the store to purchase a few cents worth of soda or tobacco. Such instances clearly illustrate how unappreciative some parents are of the value of their school.

But we do not wish to be understood as suggesting that all the fault rests with the parents. Undoubtedly in many instances the teacher is to blame for the disinterestedness and inactivity in the community. In many cases inefficient and unworthy teachers enter the profession who do not have the real good of the work at heart. Wherever this is the case we see deficient schools. A teacher is expected to be a leader in a community around whom should center the social and intellectual interests of the community. He should at all times be ready to perform any service for the advancement of the community; for he is its public servant, paid out of its public funds. He should lead instead of being led. But even the professional teacher, high in the ranks, does not always possess all of these desirable qualifications. It matters not how high may be his attainments, he should possess a character which is strong at the same time pleasing. His spirit should at all times be free from haughtiness and selfishness and his aim should be to avoid conflict between himself and his patrons and the idea of service and adaptability he should ever have with him.

So we must admit that there are duties for both parents and teacher in connection with the school. While it is the teacher's duty to make the school as pleasant and agreeable as possible and to insist at all times on a regular attendance, it is

ADVERTISEMENT FROM PAGE 6

the duty of the parents to hold up his hands by seeing that their children make this regular attendance to insist on obedience in all things. While it is the duty of the teacher to make personal visits to the homes of the patrons, to inquire into the home life of the pupils and parents and by so doing enlist the cooperation, it is the duty of the parent to reciprocate with personal visits to the school, by inquiries as to the progress of their children and to the general welfare of the school; while it is the teacher's duty to control by any legitimate means, it is the parents duty to insist on implicit obedience to all reasonable rules of the teacher; while it is the duty of the teacher to institute any forward movement for the upbuilding of the community life, it is the duty of the parents to endeavor to make his work successful; for by so doing a community service is rendered.

So by mutually working together — the parents and the teacher — a school can be unbuilded that can be a power for good in the land; a monument will be erected that will tell of service done and of advancement made. The public school is a public utility and as such is the property of every individual. It is an index to the ideals of a community, because it is just what the citizens make it. If the school is weak and the teacher inefficient, it is as the community wishes. They could have a better one if they really wanted it.

Our Mineral Wealth
(By CAPT. J. C. NELSON)

The Tennessee coal field and iron ore deposits occupy the north eastern counties of East Tennessee, which has been extensively developed throughout the entire area, showing it the equal of any alike deposits of bitumunous coal and red hemitite iron ore in commercial quality and production. Though some of these counties are farther advanced in development than Rhea county, the latter is not excelled by any of them in its massive deposits and excellent quality of products. The Dayton Coal & Iron Co. Limited, has been operating continuously for the last twenty years at Dayton two iron furnaces, of daily capacity of one hundred and fifty tons each with the Rhea county coal and iron ore. The Fox Coal Co., at Graysville, is also mining coal on a large scale and distributing the products from the Chattanooga and Atlanta markets.

The capacity of the coal and iron ore deposits in Rhea county are practically unlimited, and the why but two large industries are operated is for want of enterprise on the part of people on whom it rightfully devolved to inform capitalists, for it is amply demonstrated that operations in this field by the two companies named are profitable.

ADVERTISEMENTS FROM PAGE 6

The coal and iron ore deposits extend longitudially through the entire length of the county. The C.N.O. & T.P. railways run in close proximity to both deposits and will be easily reached at any point within the county by a spur track from the main line.

Both the coal and iron ore are easy of access and development through the entire length of the county, involving the least minimum expenditure required to put this class of industries in complete and successful operation.

[Page 7]

C., N. O. & T. P. RY.

Time Table, Effective January 11th, 1904.

NORTHBOUND	SOUTHBOUND.
No 2...10 53 am	No 1... 5 07 pm
No 4...11 37 pm	No 3... 5 21 am
No 6... 6 53 am	No 5... 6 15 pm
No 8... 6 15 pm	No 7... 7 40 am
No 84...12 15 am	No 83..12 15 am

Trains 1, 2, 8, 4, do not stop. Trains 5, 6, 7 and 8 stop at both North and South Dayton Trains 88 and 84, local freights, do not carry passengers.

H. H. Taylor, Local Agent.

DAYTON MAILS.

DECATUR.
Ar....4:80 pm | Lv....11:00 am
BIG SPRING.
Ar....9:45 am | Lv....12:80 pm
OGDEN.
Ar....4:80 pm | Lv....11:00 am

Dayton City Officials

R. M. SHERMAN, Mayor

Robt. M. Sherman was born at Ashley, Delaware county, Ohio, about fifty-one years ago, and spent his life thereabouts until he came south nineteen years ago since which he has lived continuously in this city.

Since coming to this city, Mr. Sheman has been continuously engaged in the retail grocery trade and has always enjoyed a good business. He is a man of great public spirit and manifests a keen interest in everything that promises to build up the city or develop its business.

In no sense a politician, Mr. Sherman has recently been elected mayor of the city for the fourth term and it is a common saying that "Bob" Sherman is willing to devote more of his time, talents and means to the service of his adopted city than any of his fellow townsmen.

P. T. FOUST, Recorder

Theodore Foust, or P.T. Foust as he signs himself, is a native Rhea countian, having been born in what is now the 2nd district. His father was William P. Foust.

Some sixteen years ago, Mr. Foust came to Dayton since which time he has been identified with the progress of the city. He is a lawyer by profession, but is a careful, painstaking business man as well. He is serving his third term as city recorder which position he fills with honesty and fidelity and with satisfaction to his constituency.

Since Mr. Foust is a bachelor it is not necessary that his age be revealed, though he is yet a young man. No man stands higher in the confidence of Dayton people than P.T. Foust.

W. J. LOWRY, City Marshal

W. J. Lowry, the present polite, popular and efficient marshal of the city of Dayton, was born in Bledsoe county, six miles north of Pikeville, in the year 1864. He was educated in the schools of his native county finishing the course in Sequatchie College.

He came to Dayton in 1889 where he has since resided. He served on the police force of Dayton for two years, during the wild period of the young city's growth and by his vigilance in detecting evil doers and bringing them to speedy punishment, he soon become a terror to law breakers.

He has served as city marshal for five years, and has done more to suppress crime, and convert the turbulent element into quiet, law abiding citizens than all other factors combined.

Being of a quiet, fearless and determined disposition the law breakers soon learned that he would allow no violators of the law to escape through fear or favor.

While he enforced the law vigorously and fearlessly, as an officer he has always conducted himself in a quiet, courteous, gentlemanly manner, and he today enjoys the good will, admiration and respect of all who know him.

B. B. BLEVINS

Braxton B. Blevins, or "Brack Blevins," as he is called by his friends, is one of the best known young business men of the city. His long connection with the Dayton Bank & Trust Co. has brought him in constant touch with the people of the community who have thus learned to appreciate his fine business qualities. At present he holds the position of assistant cashier of the above mentioned bank which is one of Rhea county's prosperous financial institutions.

When the city government was reorganized under the new charter in 1903, Mr. Blevins was chosen city treasurer and so well did he perform his duties and so accurately did he keep the records of the city's financial transactions that in May of the present year he was unanimously elected for another term. Before this term expires he will probably have the satisfaction of paying off the last of the city's long standing indentedness.

Mr. Blevins is an active Knight of Pythias in which order he has held several positions. He is a public spirited young man and was for several years captain of the famous Dayton Concert Band which under his leadership, won the second prize in the Chattanooga Festival band contest of 1900 over several strong competitors. The future probably holds many good things in store for Brack Blevins in the way of social, business and political advancement.

ADVERTISEMENTS FROM PAGE 7

ADVERTISEMENTS FROM PAGE 7

[Page 8]

ADVERTISING

This paper will accept advertising with the guarantee that its circulation is much larger than that of any other Rhea county paper or no charge for the service. Liberal rates will be furnished on application.

In the absence of an understanding to the contrary all advertisements will be continued until ordered out, and charged for accordingly.

Obituaries, resolutions and kindred matter will be charged for at one-half local rates.

CORRESPONDENCE

Correspondence is solicited, but every contribution should be accompanied by the true name of the author to insure its publication. This rule will be insisted upon.

ANNOUNCEMENTS

FOR CONGRESS

THE HERALD is authorized to announce Hon. M.G. Butler, of Gainsboro, a candidate for representative in congress from the Fourth district, subject to the action of the democratic party.

We are authorized to announce Hon. Alfred A. Adams, of Lebanon, Wilson county, as a Candidate for Congress in this the Fourth Congressional District, subject to the action of the Democratic party.

Dayton, Friday, June 24, 1904

VOLUME VII, NUMBER 1

It has been our purpose for some time to issue some sort of a special edition on the occasion of our sixth anniversary and the same is now before you. It is not so complete as we could wish or even as we had intended to make it, but we offer neither complaints nor apologies.

We desire here to record our thanks for the assistance rendered in the preparation of matter by Cols. V.C. Allen, W.L. Givens, Prof. W.E. Stephens, Mr. H.A. Crawford, Supt. Frazier, Capt. J.C. Nelson and others, and especially to Mr. D.J. Ogilvie for his untiring efforts in aiding us to get views for use in the illustrations.

At another time we hope to present you with something better worth while.

EVERY teacher attending the Normal should purchase and send home a copy of THE HERALD special.

================

THE political grafter has again made his appearance in our midst, but is said to be receiving scant attention from the various candidates.

================

SHERIFF W.P. HAYS, of Hamilton county, nominated by the republicans for re-election last Saturday withdrew from the race on account of the organization of the county committee by those indifferent to his interests.

================

THE announcement of J.T. Crawford as a candidate for trustee appears elsewhere in this paper. Lack of space prevents an extended notice here, but we shall have more to say of the matter later. Jim excels greatly in point of business qualifications for the duties of the office — not the least consideration in choosing an official.

Peabody State Institute

Pursuant to previous arrangements, the Peabody State Institute for this section of the state met in the court house at 10 a.m. June 20th. The institute was called to order by Chairman Fred B. Frazier, superintendent of Public Instruction for Rhea county. In an eloquent address the chairman fully explained the object of the gathering and then called upon the conductor and instructors of the institute all of whom responded in pleasing talks, each outlining his work. Talks were had by Rev. G.W. Brewer, Esq. J.L. Henry, W.E. Stephens and others.

The Institute then adjourned to meet in the evening session at 7:45 p.m. at which time the following program was rendered:

PROGRAM

Chorus by choir — Miss Ethel Blevins, pianist.

Invocation — Rev. W. N. Price.

Instrumental solo — Miss Clark Haggard.

Introductory remarks — Supt. Fred B. Frazier.

Address of welcome — J. L. Henry, R.M. Sherman and W.E. Stephens.

Response to address of welcome — R.L. Jones, superintendent of Hamilton county public schools.

Instrumental solo — Miss Carrie Stephens.

Address by Superintendent S.G. Gilbreath, Hon. B.G. McKenzie, Superintendent M.R.M. Burke.

The attendance at this social meeting was immense, the enthusiasm great.

SUPERINTENDENT
S.G. GILBREATH,
Conductor

SUPERINTENDENT
M.R.M BURKE
Instructor

The enrollment Monday was entirely satisfactory and many others came Tuesday. Miss Maude Chandler, who has charge of primary methods and physical culture, did not arrive till Monday evening.

Prof. C.K. Gallaher, superintendent of Meigs county public schools, and principal of Meigs county high school, addressed the institute Tuesday in a short but able discourse.

The evening session of Tuesday was occupied in a public reception given in honor of faculty and "out of town" teachers and superintendents. J.L. Godsey was chairman of the reception committee. A copious rain shower at sunset somewhat interfered with this entertainment, but it was a pleasant and profitable session.

Vocal solos at intervals between periods of intense hand shakings, smiles and felicitous greetings were given for the future cheer and merriment of the occasion were given by Misses Ida Hixon and Bertha L. Ferguson of Pikeville.; Misses Imogene Woollen, Bertie Eaves, Clark Haggard and Carrie Stephens of Dayton.

Some of the prominent "out of county" educators attending institute are as follows:

E.A. Lowery, of Granville, Jackson county; M.L. Morrison, Joel Rogers, E.F. Bell, Hamilton county; Miss Sallie Bates, Tasso; Miss Dollie Bryant, Charleston; O.W. Barnes, Apison; B.D. Hill, Hill City; Miss Eugene Coulter, Stephens Chapel; Miss Maude Fain, Cleveland; J.W. Barnes, Verdie; Miss Mary Henderson, Charleston; Miss Martha Juve, Watburg; Rice J. Wesley, Climer; Miss Mildred J. Stevens, East Lake; J.T. Smith, Igou's Ferry; Miss Etta Wade, St. Elmo; Elbert Wattenbarger, Athens; J.S. Ziegler, Sale Creek; W.J. Ziegler, Highland Park.

Prof. Wm. Renegan, Geo. A. Shipley and Miss Bertha Ferguson, of Pikeville, are at the institute.

TIME OF INSTITUTE
June 20 — July 17. Daily sessions from 8:30 a.m. to 3:30 p.m. 5 days in week.

FACULTY
S. G. Gilbreath, conductor.

M. R. M. Burke,   B. O. Duggan,

R. L. Jones,   Miss Maude Chandler.

At chapel services this Wednesday morning addresses were delivered by Prof. J.C. Fooshee, city; and G.A. Fooshee, At'ty. I.T.

SUPT. FRED B. FRAZIER

Fred B. Frazier, superintendent of Rhea county schools, is only twenty-five or twenty-six years old, but has made for himself an enviable reputation in the great work he has done in awakening interest in the cause of public education. News of what has been accomplished here has spread every where until his name is a familiar one in educational circles all over the state. It was through his intelligent foresight and powers of organization that the present Peabody Institute was located here.

For the most part, Mr. Frazier was educated in the public schools and at Tennessee Valley College. In 1900, he obtained a Peabody scholarship and spent two years at Nashville equipping himself for his chosen work of teaching. He is said to be quite a handsome young man.

ADVERTISEMENT FROM PAGE 8

ADVERTISEMENTS FROM PAGE 8

[Page 9]

LOCAL and PERSONAL
Items of Interest Picked-Up Here and There

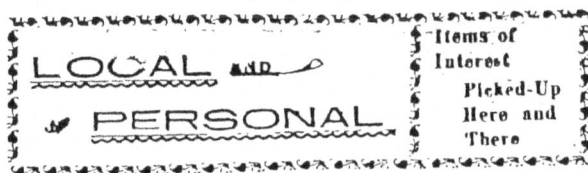

How do you like it?

Phone 33 for livery outfits.

Lawn Mowers at A. Johnson & Sons.

C.L. Moon, of Birchwood, was in the city Monday.

John Neal, of Rhea Springs, was in the city Monday.

Call on D.R. Bolen for oak and heart pine shingles.

Screen doors and windows any size at A. Johnson & Sons.

P.C. Tallent spent Sunday with friends at Spring City.

Creed Cunnyngham was down from Spring City Tuesday.

Hon. Creed F. Bates, of Chattanooga, was in the city Tuesday.

W.B. Benson and son Ed, spent Sunday at Rhea Springs.

A few more copies of the anniversary special at 5 cents each.

W.Y. Denton and J.L. Burnett, of Montague, were here Tuesday.

Mr. and Mrs. James Robeson visited relatives at Decatur Sunday.

Miss Eva McDonald, of Harriman, visited friends here last Sunday.

Miss Bernice Miller, of Morristown, is visiting relatives here this week.

The Presbyterian Sunday school enjoyed a picnic to the gulch Tuesday.

We have cut the prices all to pieces on men's pants.   N.D. REED & SON.

T.D. Burkhalter, of Shamrock, Tex., was the guest of his brother here this week.

Claude McDonald and Spence Deakins, of Pikeville, were in the city Tuesday.

Deputy U.S. Marshal W.B. Spears, of Jasper, spent several days in the city this week.

The ice-cream supper of the Sunbeam Society Tuesday evening netted the sum of $23.

Spring is a splendid time at which to be merry over J.F. Henninger's bargains.

THE HERALD and the American Home Journal — a splendid magazine — one year 60¢.

Wanted — Hens, frying chickens and eggs, highest cash prices paid by J.D. Burkhalter.

Prove the way to comfort by buying a pair of Douglass Shoes at J.F. Henninger's.

Dr. A.L. King and daughter, Miss Joe, of Athens, spent several days of this week with friends here.

Mrs. T.S. Kennedy, of Newport, Ky., is the guest of her sister, Mrs. W.S. Greer, on south Market street.

The boys' pants at J.F. Henninger's are strong and thick just where you and Johnny will appreciate this quality.

The largest and best stock of Ladies Mens and Childrens Shoes and Slippers at J.F. Henningers that ever came to Dayton.

I.C. Arrants, of Decatur, accompanied by his charming daughters, Misses Mary and Alex, were guests of relatives here last Sunday.

You are cordially invited to attend the great exposition of Dry Goods, Clothing, and Shoes at J.F. Henninger's popular store.

Messrs. Tallent and Vance, republican candidates for trustee and sheriff, have been to the woods in pursuit of the voters this week.

Dr. W.B. Williams will move a portion of his family to Rhea Springs for the summer, and while at the springs the doctor will engage in the practice of his profession.

Geo. A. Fooshee, formerly a citizen of Dayton, but now a leading lawyer of Coalgate, Ind. Ter., was the guest of his brother, Prof. J.C. Fooshee, here this week.

Send your friends a copy of the extra.

Get your livery from Williamson & Darwin.

THE HERALD 50 cents cash; 75 cents on time.

Brooks & Kelly Furniture and Undertaking.

Easy prcesi [sic] for easy suspenders at J. F. Henninger's.

Get a Blue Grass Razor on Trial at A. Johnson & Sons.

Satisfaction is a practice not a theory with us.   J.F. HENNINGER

FOR SALE — Two Jersey cows. Apply to R.S. Colbaugh, Dayton, Tenn.

THE HERALD and Southern Fruitgrower for 80 cents cash at this office.

A big lot of $1.50 and $1.35 shoes now goes at $1.00 at N.D. Reed & Son.

You get more and better goods at J.F. Henninger's than you can find elsewhere.

Unless a man drops dead he will surely see the great bargains in J.F. Henninger's clothing.

Master Wendall Harden, of Spring City, is the guest of his grandparents, Mr. and Mrs. A. Johnson, this week.

J.N. Ewing and D.M. Rhea, of Spring City, attended the democratic committee meeting here last Saturday.

If you are going on a summer trip provide yourself with a pair or two of those easy slippers at J.F. Hnninger's.

J.F. Henninger is better prepared with the largest and cheapest of goods he has ever had for the berry trade.

Can't be perfect health without pure blood. Burdeck Blood Bitters makes pure blood. Tones and invigorates the whole system.

Mr. and Mrs. G.T. Atchley, of Oakland, Cal., were guests of the former's mother and sister, Mrs. E.F. and Miss Lizzie Atchley, in this city for a few days the past week.

Summer Tourist tickets now on sale via Queen & Crescent Route to points north. For information, in regard to same, address ticket agent or G. E. CLARKE, T.P.A., LEXINGTON, KY.

Don't sell your hens, frying chickens and eggs for merchandise when you can get the same price in cash from J.D. Burkhalter, corner 1st Ave. and Market St.

Mothers lose their dread for "that terrible second summer" when they have Dr. Fowler's Extract of Wild Strawberry in the house. Nature's specific for bowel complaint of every sort.

All the diseases start in the bowels. Keep them open or you will be sick. CASCARETS act like nature. Keep liver and bowels active without a sickening griping feeling. Six million people take and recommend CASCARETS. Try a 10¢ box. All druggist.

At a meeting of the city school board last night the following teachers were elected: Prof. J.C. Fooshee, Pricipal; Mrs. Edna Benson, Misses Kate Knight, Ethel Blevins, and Etta Buttler, of Harriman.

Notice was received this week that Manager Ernest Williams, of the local telephone exchange, would be transferred to a similar position at Bristol so soon as his place here could be filled. Dayton people will be sorry to lose Mr. and Mrs. Williams.

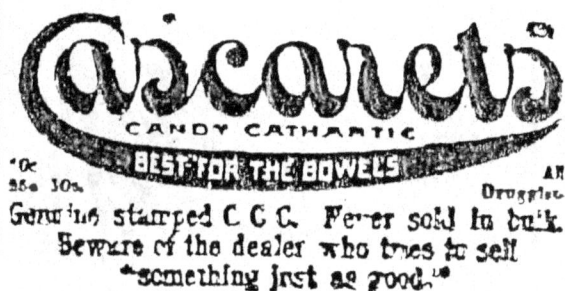

ADVERTISEMENT FROM PAGE 9

FIRST BAPTIST PICNIC

The Sunday School of the First Baptist church enjoyed a most delightful outing down on Big Richland yesterday. More than two hundred of all ages went and spent a merry, happy day.

The D. C. & I. Co. very generously furnished their train to convey everybody to the grounds and, after the day was far spent, took them to see the beautiful Tennessee and from thence to the mines and back to the city.

Every one was loud in his praise of the Company for its courtesy and especially to Messers. Barton and Wilbur for their efforts which contributed so much to the pleasure of the outing.

Institute Entertainment

Monday, June 27th, 9:30

Chorus.

Invocation — Rev. Simmons.

Instrumental Duet— Mrs. Lester Woollen and Imogene Woollen.

Reading — Edwina Taylor.

Instrumental Solo — Mrs. Frank Jackson.

Address — Prof. B. O. Duggan.

Vocal Solo — Miss Mildred Stephens.

Reading — Miss Lena Morgan.

Chorus — Choir.

S. H. Pearcy

S.H. Pearcy, our enterprising undertaker and manufacturer of tombstones, is greatly improving the looks of his Market street property by painting and otherwise adding repairs.

His display of monuments is quite an attraction and under a new fence that is now built, these premises add much to the beauty of the surroundings.

Mr. Pearcy is one of our most energetic business men.

Church Services

Preaching at the First Presbyterian church at 11 a.m. and 7:45 p.m. Subject for the morning, Is not this the Christ? Evening, The Foolishness of the Plan. Mrs. Ernest Williams will sing at these services.

Preaching at Wilkie & Shelton's blacksmith shop Saturday at 3 p.m. The old songs will be sung and the old time religion preached. Every body come.

Every person who gets their laundry done at the Chattanooga Steam Laundry will get a chance on a ticket with all expences paid to St. Louis. A chance in every package. Save your laundry and tickets for John Gilbreath.

ADVERTISEMENTS FROM PAGE 9

The City of Dayton, A Descriptive Sketch

(By PROF. W. E. STEPHENS)

On the 14th day of March, 1885, the legal voters of Dayton, once called Smith's X Roads, voted to incorporate said place as "The Town, or City of Dayton," by a vote of 120 to 12, the total voting population at that time as per list, being 175. On the 18th day of March, 1885, the charter was granted; the first mayor was T.N.L. Cunnyngham; first recorder, W.B. Benson.

In 1895, a new charter was obtained by special act of the legislature with the corporate name, "City of Dayton." In 1903, amendments were made to said charter eliminating some of the then included territory and adding other territory.

LOCATION

Dayton is located in the valley of East Tennessee, 38 miles north of Chattanooga, near Walden's Ridge, on the west, and about 3 miles from the Tennessee river, on the east. It is traversed north and south by the Cincinnati Southern Railroad, west and east by the famous Richland creek. To the southwest, almost within "a stones throw," stands the historic Lone mountain.

ENTERPRISES

May 9, 1884, the Dayton Coal & Iron Co. took the initial steps in the erection of two large blast furnaces with a capacity each of 150 tons pr day. These furnaces have been a successful operation since their erection save now and then a cesation of a few weeks for repairs.

The five story building of the Dayton Milling Co. has recently been moved to a location near the C.S. railway. The capacity for the manufacture of flour is 125 barrels per day and a bushel of meal per minute. The officers of the company are: J.W. Hudson, pres. and gen. manager; T.N. Henderson, sec. and treas.; E.N. Keith, miller. Brands of flour, "Magnolia," "King of Patents," "Daisy," "Whiter than Snow," "Red Log."

The Black Haw Medicine Co., in a three story brick building near new depot, is actively engaged in the manufacture of various valuable medicines. J.T. Deanger is president of company and Frank McDonald, business manager.

Dayton has a foundary, two banks, two manufacturers of soft drinks, two drug stores, five or more furniture stores, some fifteen or more dry goods and grocery stores, two weekly news papers and such other conveniences as are found in other towns of 3,000 inhabitants.

CHURCHES

The following churches in Dayton have pastors and regular services: First Baptist, Second Baptist, Presbyterian, Cumberland Presbyterian, Methodist Episcopal, Methodist Episcopal South, Christian.

There are also three churches for colored people.

SCHOOLS

Dayton has a system of city schools open eight months in the year, doing admirable work with Prof. Fooshee as superintendent with six other teachers for white schools and three for colored schools. These schools have three departments: Primary, Grammar, and High School. The High School course is about the same as is used in cities.

Dayton Masonic College, Douglas High School, Dayton University and Dayton Classical Institute played each in its turn a prominent part in the education of the youths of Dayton and vicinity, but now the work is being done in Dayton's graded public schools and "in going abroad."

ADDENDA

The Creator has dealt generously, even lavishly, with the section of country of which Dayton is the geographical and commercial center. In the wealth and variety of its natural resources it is not excelled, if indeed it is equaled, by any community in the south. With coal and iron ore by millions of tons at her very door, with almost untouched virgin forests of the various species of commercial timbers in close proximity, with the finest limestone in the land in exhaustless quantities, with numerous unerring indications of oil, zinc and other undeveloped minerals, with a fruit belt the variety and richness of whose products rival the famous fields of California, with a soil that yields annual and abundant crops of all the leading cereals, legumes and grasses, with its equable climate, its healthful, life-giving atmosphere and its pure, cold spring water, the people of this section can well afford to smile at the benignity of Providence and contemplate the future with a feeling of serene confidence. To them the problem of life appears an easy one. They have but to put forth their hands to grasp untold wealth. And if in its virgin profusion they are confused and overwhelmed they have but to invite the attention of the world to have thousands come in to share in its development, production and enjoyment

* * *

Within less than one mile from the corporate limits of Dayton during the season of 1903 one man gathered from twelve acres of land a crop of strawberries which he marketed for $2,800, yielding him a net profit above all expenditures of about $150 an acre. During the present season with less than a half crop the product of another acre was marketed for $111.25. These yields,while by no means exceptional but quite common, are pointers which indicate the possibilities of the business.

* * *

The peach crop of Rhea county for 1904 will probably be the largest in its history.

Dayton Coal & Iron Company

Among the great industries that contribute materially to the progress and prosperity of the south the furnaces of the D.C. & I. Co. and tributary industries dependent on their successful operation are by no means an unimportant factor.

These twin stacks each of 200 tons cap. are 75 ft. high and form an imposing structure in striking contrast with the methods of Tubal-Cain, standing out, as they do in bold relief against the verdant and picturesque slopes of Lone Mountain as a fitting back ground.

These stacks are advantageously located surrounded as they are by an illimitable and inexhaustible supply of mineral wealth containing all the prerequisites essential to the manufacture of a high grade of southern pig. They give employment to hundreds of men and have quite recently added new and modern improvements to the plant entailing an aggregate expense of $100,000.

Just to the north-west is located the celebrated Nelson mine producing hundreds of tons of coal daily peculiarily adapted to the manufacture of coke in 375 ovens owned and operated by the company.

Further up the gulch formed by parallel mountains we find the "Laurel Creek" and "Richland mines" forming in combination one of the most valuable and extensive coal fields in the south. Considerable geological importance is attached to this great coal area. The Nelson division is especially abounding in geological interests owing to its peculiar structure and formation, nature as though in a capricous mood seems to have darted hither and thither bending, coiling and twisting into multitudious forms; one place you find a normal face of coal 4 to 8 ft. while a little further on, perchance, it broadens out to 25 ft. in thickness.

The major portion of the ore used is mined from their mine known as "The Crescent." This mine is located at Knott, Tenn.; the ore is transported on barges down the Tennessee river to the Co. docks at the mouth of Richland Creek where it is tansferred by means of hoisting machinery to the Company cars to be unloaded ready for use on the fevors of the stock-house.

The "crescent" is a hard fossiliferous ore and carries a sufficiently high percent of lime to constitute a self fluxing ore quite an advantage in manipulation as well as the means of saving a considerable sum.

These furnaces have been in operation almost continuously since their completion in 1884, the product of these furnaces owing to its great adaptibility to a high class of work is in demand among foundry men and manufacturers.

Mr. M. H. Maury holds the position of general manager of the local plant.

The success of his administration under the trying circumstances of adverse conditions brought about by the tendency to decline and depression in the iron market bespeaks for him a judicious sense of fairness and diplomatic finesse that has made him unanimously popular, alike with the citizen and working men.

One of the most interesting and important features of the business is the mammoth department store established by the company for the convenience of their employees.

This store is managed by Mr. W.A. Ault, a comparatively young man well and favorably known through out Rhea county. Mr. Ault brought into this work the same energy and enthusiasm manifested in the transaction of his own affairs. Mr. Ault has introduced new men and new methods and in many ways departed from old lines, greatly reducing prices on every thing handled.

Mr. Ault has installed an ice house and delivers ice to the doors of his patrons each day.

The meat market run in connection with the store keeps a constant supply of fresh meats.

A visit to this hive of industry is interesting and instructive, while its systematic, economical and business like management with one attention to all details would prove a revelation to a student of political economy or an agitator of municipal ownership.

The Dayton Milling Company

In November 1899, J.W. Hudson and associates acquired the Dayton Flour Mill Company property located at the county bridge, little Richland Creek, which was operated continuously until January 1st, 1904.

At this time the management determined to move the buildings to a splended site formerly occupied by the Gem City Mill Co., on the C.N.O. & T.P. Ry., and install an entirely new line of machinery.

J.W. HUDSON

Accordingly the contract was awarded the Nordyke & Marmon Co., Indianapolis, Ind., one of the worlds largest mill builders, to install the best 100-barrel flour and 600-bushels corn mills they could build.

The plant was completed and began operation May 1st. In the mean time a new company was organized and chartered under the name Dayton Milling Co., capital stock $30,000. J. W. Hudson president and general manager, T. N. Henderson secretary and treasurer.

The cut appearing on the cover of this paper [see page 27, this publication. B.J.B.] shows the mill and storage warehouse for 15,000 bushels of grain, equipped with elevators and conveyors for handling the grain from cars. The mill has ample side track which gives splendid shipping facilities.

They will require annually a large amount of grain which affords a market at home for all the grain in this and adjoining counties. In many ways this substantial enterprise is a benefit to the city and section.

The mill does a merchant and exchange business, their product is proving satisfactory, the owners are very much pleased with their new mill, and the future for them seems bright.

Dayton Bank & Trust Co.

The Dayton Bank & Trust company, under the efficient management and control of J.P. Dean cashier, and B.B. Blevins, assistant cashier, is regarded as one of the substantial commercial institutes of Rhea county, and its business is constantly growing in volume and importance.

The three most important factors in all commercial transactions are reliability, promptness, and efficiency and these are the points that make up and constitute the strength and popularity of the Dayton Bank & Trust Co.

The business transacted by this bank throughout the entire year is very great; but during the fruit and berry season it is something enormous.

With ample capital, wide connections throughout the South, liberal terms and curteous treatment, this bank enjoys the patronage of the best and most successful business men of the county.

ADVERTISEMENTS FROM PAGE 10

[Page 11]

JOHN ABEL

Mr. John Abel is one of Dayton's most thrifty and enterprising business men in addition to being a thoroughly polite, courteous and highly polished gentleman. He possesses a sense of rare taste and tackfulness that enables him to cater to the different classes of trade in a manner and after a fashion characteristic of the most successful business men.

Mr. Abel was never in a better position to cater to the wants of a scrupulous and exacting public than at present. In addition to a thorough and complete line of fancy and staple groceries, he has the tastiest, toniest [*sic*] most elegant and strictly up-to-date line of clothes, watches, musical instruments and jewelry ever placed for the inspection of town and county trade.

When we consider the fact that Mr. Abel pays out more money to the farmers and country people in connection with lumber, cross ties and fencing contracts with the C.S. Ry. than any business man in Rhea or adjoining counties, it cannot be gain sayed that he is a public benefactor.

Therefore it behooves the people of this section to rally around Mr. Abel to support and encourage him with your patronage. "Help the man that helps you is a sure road to a more bountiful prosperity."

So complete is Mr. Abel's line of shoes, clothing, and notions that the sorriest tramp the country ever produced might walk in one door of his mammoth department store and although he possessed only a nominal sum, come out of the other a polished gentleman.

"A maximum quantity and quality of all the needs and necessity of the human family at a minimum cost" is his business motto and is strictly adherred to whether his patron be the simplest child or the shrewdest of bargainers, one price to all is a rule he keeps inviolate.

Mr. Abel has recently purchased the entire block in which his business is located and contemplates putting in a thoroughly, complete and strictly up-to-date line of hardware, farming implements and etc., the coming fall.

We dare say in view of his energetic and successful efforts and business like policies of the past that this line will defy all competition along the line of low prices, high quality and unequaled completeness.

Bank Statement

Report of the conditions of the American National Bank in Dayton in the State of Tennessee, at the close of business, June 9, 1904.

RESOURCES

Loans and Discounts	$89,527.56
Overdrafts, secured & unsecured	700.14
U.S. Bonds to secure circulation	7,000.00
Premium on U.S. Bonds	350.00
Bonds, securities, etc.	458.62
Banking house, furniture & fixtures	1,053.50
Due from National Bank (not reserve agents)	13,773.76
Due from approved reserve agents	7,847.99
Checks and other cash items	461.24
Notes of other National Banks	60.00
Fractional paper currency, nickles and cents	100.47
Specie 5,023	
Legal-tender notes 3,470	
	8,493.00
Redemption fund with U.S. Treasurer (5% of circulation)	350.00
Total	130,176.28

LIABILITIES

Capital stock paid in	$25,000.00
Surplus fund	7,000.00
Undivided profits, less expenses and taxes paid	2,164.27
National Bank notes outstanding	7,000.00
Individual deposits subject to check	64,200.42
Demand certificates of deposit	24,736.72
Cashier's checks outstanding	65.87
Total	130,176.28

STATE OF TENNESSEE, COUNTY OF RHEA

I, F.R. Rogers, Cashier of the above named bank, do solemnly swear that the above statement is true to the best of my knowledge and belief.   F. R. ROGERS, Cashier

Subscribed and sworn to before me this 17 day of June, 1904. B. G. McKENZIE
                    Notary Public

Correct Attest:
    A. P HAGGARD
    J. H. ROGERS   Directors
    W. H. ROGERS

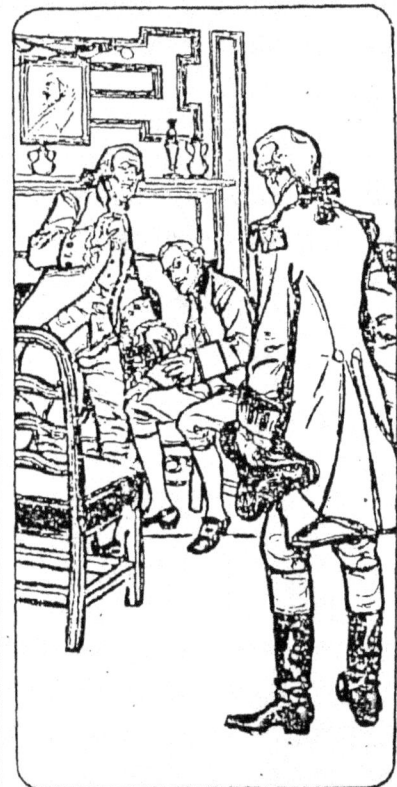

HEARTS COURAGEOUS By HALLIE ERMINIE RIVES

Copyright 1902 by The Bowen-Merrill Company

[Page 12]

Birchwood

Birchwood, June 21 — Mrs. Taliaferro spent Tuesday with friends near Georgetown.

W.N. Knox, of Knoxville, visited our merchants Wednesday.

Miss Lillie Anderson, of Georgetown, was the guest of friends here Tuesday night.

Miss Maggie Witt is visiting relatives in Chattanooga.

William Hodge spent Thursday and Friday in Chattanooga.

Miss Colwell, of Cleveland, is visiting relatives near this place.

A.J. Gross and W. Roark made a business trip to Chattanooga Saturday.

Willie Weir was over from Evensville Sunday.

Jeff Davis, of Harrison, visited friends here Sunday.

Mr. and Mrs. J.G. Lane and son, of Shepard, are visiting the former's parents at this place.

Miss Edith Bare, of Sherman Heights, spent a few days of last week with her mother here.

Morris Gross was over from Big Spring Sunday.

Reece Bare and children, of Sherman Heights, visited relatives here last week.

Spring City

Spring City, June 21. — Miss Maude Elliott returned Wednesday from a pleasant visit in Chattanooga.

R. Baker returned Wednesday from St. Louis.

Messrs. Watt Johnson, P.C. Tallent, Jesse Goodrich, Claude Givens, Braxton Blevins, Carl Whitener and W.B. Benson, of Dayton, were in town Sunday.

Mr. and Mrs. John Wheelock were guests of relatives here Sunday.

Mrs. Randell, of Chattanooga, is visiting her son, Joe Randell.

Mr. and Mrs. W.M. Cate spent Sunday in Rhea Springs.

Mrs. Brown, of Chattanooga, is the guest of her daughter, Mrs. Randell.

Sheffield

Geo. Smith, who is working at Knott, visited home folks Sunday.

Clarance Palmer is visiting relatives in Chattanooga.

Mr. and Mrs. J.A. DeVaney, of Evensville, visited here last week.

Dr. R.C. Miller and wife, of Evensville, were here this week.

J.L. DeVaney made a business trip to Spring City Monday.

Dr. J.R. Hoover, of Dayton, is visiting friends at this place.

Willie Rogers, of Sherman Heights, spent a few days with relatives here this week.

White Beard has purchased a new buggy.

Miss Tenny Miller, of Dayton, is visiting her parents at this place.

W.C. Eberly attended an ice cream supper at Evensville last week.

Quite a number of people from this place attended Childrens Day exercises at Johns Chapel Sunday.

The Sunday School is making preparations for a childrens day here Sunday but no dinner on the ground.

REPUBLICANS of Knox county will nominate no tickest for the August election leaving the democratic factions to fight it out.

==============

HAVING made his peace with Brownlow, the Hon. Dana Harmon was on last Saturday nominated for attorney general to succeed the late S.B. Keefauver, of the First circuit.

==============

RHEA county has not had the pleasure of voting for a gentleman more capable of properly filling a seat in the legislature in twenty years than Hon. J.W. Lillard, a sketch of whom appears elsewhere.

MAKE IT PUBLIC

Publicity counts, that's What the people want. Dayton expression on the subject

Make it public. Tell the people about it. Gratitude promotes publicity. Grateful citizens talk. They tell their neighbors; tell their friends. The news is too good to keep. "Bad news" are numerous. So few understand the cause. Many Dayton people are learning. And better still, they are being cured. Lame backs are lame no more. Weak ones regain their strength.

This is the every-day labor in Dayton. Of Doan's Kidney Pills. Our citizens are making it public. Here's a case of it:

J.A. Bryant of Third Ave., a retired groceryman says: "Doan's Kidney Pills first came to my notice by seeing them advertised in a Grand Rapids newspaper and I sent to Chattanooga to get a box. My condition at the time was quite bad and I suffered from a dull aching in the small of my back. The kidney secretions were to frequent and highly colored. I have derived much benefit from Doan's Kidney Pills and I think them an excellent remedy. I do not hesitate to recommend readers here in Dayton to procure them at Cunnyngham's drug store and give them a fair trial."

For sale by all dealers, price 50 cents. Foster-Milburn Co., Buffalo, N.Y. sole agents for the United States. Remember the name Doan's and take no substitute.

COL. J. G. M. MONTGOMERY, late commander of the 5th Tenn. Confederate regiment, died at Cartersville, Ga., Sunday night the 12th instant. Col. Montgomery was well known to some of our old soldiers many of whom served under him.

A Puzzle Worth Having

Dr. G.G. Green, of Woodbury, New Jersey, whose advertisement appears in our paper regularly, will mail to any one sending a two-cent stamp to pay postage, one of his new German Syrup and August Flower Puzzles, made of wood and glass. It amuses and perplexes young and old. Although very difficult, it can be mastered. Mention this paper.

ROOSEVELT AND FAIRBANKS

---o---

Nominated by Republican Convention at Chicago

The republican national convention terminated its labors at Chicago yesterday with the nomination of Theodore Roosevelt for president and Charles W. Fairbanks, of Indiana, for vice-president.

The platform "stands pat" on the doctrine of protection, deals out fulsome praise for the republican administration and threatens to reduce southern representation in congress on account of franchise regulations.

DEMOCRATS ORGANIZE

---o---

Preliminary Meeting of the County Committee Here Last Saturday

Pursuant to agreement reached at the Spring City convention the members of the democratic county committee met at the court house last Saturday to organize and discuss plans for the campaign which is now opening.

After a thorough canvass of the situation Dr. W.M. Snyder, of Spring City, was chosen chairman and Euclid Waterhouse, of rural route No. 2, vice-chairman of the committee. A.N. Grice was elected secretary pro tem.

Mr. Waterhouse tendered his resignation as chairman of the 4th district which was accepted and E.M. Williamson chosen to succeed him.

Have You a Cough?

A dose of Ballard's Horehound Syrup will relieve it. Have you a cold? A dose of Herbine at bed time and frequent small doses of Horehound Syrup during the day will remove it. Try it for whooping cough, for asthma, for consumption, for bronchitis. . . . 25c 50c $1.00 at J.R. Cunnyngham's.

ADVERTISEMENT FROM PAGE 12

District Convention

The democrats of the 3rd district met at the court house last Saturday afternoon to nominate candidates for the district offices. B.G. McKenzie was elected chairman and A.N. Grice secretary.

The names of J.F. Dosson and J.C. Carney were placed in nomination and both were nominated by acclamation. J.H. Jewell was also nominated for tax assessor by acclamation.

The meetng them adjourned.

For Trustee

TO THE VOTERS OF RHEA COUNTY:

Having been nominated for trustee I hereby announce my candidacy for said office and solicit the influence and support of all voters promising an impartial and efficient discharge of my duties if elected.   J.T. CRAWFORD

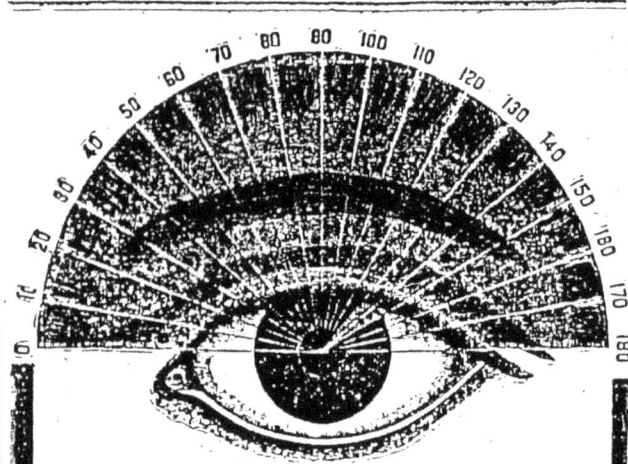
ADVERTISEMENTS FROM PAGE 12

ADVERTISEMENT FROM PAGE 12

[Page 13]

THE WEEKLY HERALD

F.M. MORRISON

THE HERALD was established in June 1898 by Morrison & Painter, but soon thereafter passed to the control of the senior partner, Mr. F.M. Morrison, who was a veteran in the ranks of Tennessees journalism. Although there were at the time three other papers published in the city, THE HERALD soon achieved a position of influence in the community. In its early youth it was called upon to stand by the grave of two of its rivals, and while the other has contrived to maintain a rather fitful existence it has required the services of several diffferent doctors to prevent the departure of the flickering spark of vitality.

T.J. CAMPBELL

May 1, 1900, T.J. Campbell and T.A. Gross purchased and assumed control of the plant and good will of the HERALD, and continued in the business about two years, Mr. Gross retiring from the firm. Mr. Campbell then became the proprietor and has since guided the destinies of the paper. He was ably assisted for a time by Mr. W.J. Black, who now holds a responsible position with an Atlanta printing establishment.

Early in the present year, Mr. Claude R. Givens became connected with the paper in the capacity of city editor, a position he has filled with ability and efficiency. The balance of the office force who have contributed to the work on this special edition are J.B. CAMPBELL, foreman, Miss Maggie Dosson, chief compositor, Misses Lizzie Atchley and Parrie Campbell compositors.

The publication of THE HERALD was begun on an Army press and every printer knows what that means. Later an Idea Cylinder was used until within the past few months the increase in the size and business of the paper made necessary the installation of a Cincinnati Drum Cylinder press and an Anderson gasoline engine.

C.R. GIVENS

When the present management assumed control of the paper the supply of type was deficient in quantity and worn-out in quality. Every pound of body type has since been renewed and more than one hundred pounds added. Besides some fifteen or twenty fonts of a new job type have been added as well as numerous other necessary modern fixtures.

The management of THE HERALD supports the principles of the democratic party as a matter of choice, and not as a party organ controlled by some boss or ring. The editors of the paper have convictions and do not mind to express them. The paper dares to contend for who is right regardless of party or caucus. Its course in this respect has won for it the confidence of the people of Rhea county and brought to it its great increase in circulation and business. It has led in every reform movement in the city or county since its establishment — many resulting from its initiative. It has had part in the following reforms, most of them already accomplished or in the process of consumation:

1. The redistricting of the county by act of the legislature.
2. The closing of the doors of Dayton saloons.
3. Eliminating of saloon influence from county politics.
4. The cessation of warfare against the Dayton Coal & Iron Co.
5. The payment of a salary to the county superintendent along with the requirement that he earn it.
6. The establishment of rural school libraries.
7. The unification of the city schools under one management.
8. The organization of Dayton business men to promote the interests of the city.

JAMES S. FRAZIER

James S. Frazier, who was nominated for sheriff by the democrats at the Spring City convention, is in the bloom of a splendid manhood. Born on his father's farm near Washington about twenty-nine years ago, he has lived there all his life which has been spent in farming and stock raising. His education was obtained in the public schools of the neighborhood, in the Dayton city schools and the Tennessee Valley College at Evensville.

There is probably today no better known or more universally popular young man in Rhea county than Jim Frazier. By dint of hard work and good judgment in trading he has achieved something of a success in a business way. And his cool head, quick judgment and steady nerve promise to make him one of the best peace officers in this part of the state.

Mr. Frazier enters the race for sheriff with a clean record and with nothing to apologize for. There isn't a speck on his reputation to which an opponent can point to his detriment. His life is an open book known and read of all men. Having been named by his party as its choice for sheriff he earnestly seeks the support of all voters assuring all of his purpose to conduct a clean, honorable, manly canvass.

Cherishing since boyhood an ambition to fill the office of sheriff and possessing every qualification necessary to a proper discharge of its duties, Mr. Frazier naturally feels in view of the wide spread demand for his nomination quite confident of election. He has many assurances to this effect from members of both parties for which he is very grateful and in return for which he promises to make a record of which his friends will not feel ashamed.

J. T. CRAWFORD

James T. Crawford was born at Washington in 1869 and is therefore thirty-five years old. He was raised on a farm and attended the county schools in winter. During the year 1889, he was bookkeeper for the Cherokee Medicine Company which was then doing business in this city.

Later, he attended the University of Tennessee until 1891 and immediately after leaving school accepted a position as timekeeper for the Dayton Coal & Iron Company.

ADVERTISEMENT FROM PAGE 13

During his service with the Dayton Coal & Iron Company, Mr. Crawford was promoted to the position of bookkeeper and for several years had charge of one [of] their principal payrolls. He resigned his position with this company last year to devote his attention to his expanding business. He has been engaged in the drug business for several years with John M. Storie in charge of the prescription department, and has built up a large trade.

The subject of this sketch is a son of H.A. Crawford, for many years a magistrate and chairman of the county court. He is a splendid penman, an expert bookkeeper and one of the best business men in Rhea county. A native son of Rhea, and proud of it, he is extremely popular with all classes of people. The nomination of Mr. Crawford for trustee by the democrats a few days since gives assurance of reclaiming that office from the republicans by whom it has been held for several years.

HON. E. P. TIPTON
Mine Inspector

The subject of this sketch was born September 20, 185-[sic], at Altamont, Grundy county, where he spent the first seventeen years of his life. Receiving such education as the common schools afforded he later supplemented this with a course in the mining schools of Pennsylvania. This has been still further developed and added to by travel and experiences as a miner and mine official in nearly all the great mining centers of the Middle, Southern and Western states, territories and Mexico.

Entering the service of the Tennessee Coal, Iron & Railway Co. at the age of seventeen, Mr. Tipton has been engaged in mining in some of its phases continuously since. And while it is probably true that no man of his age has had a wider experience in mining, he is still a student and expects to remain such.

Mr. Tipton was appointed district mine inspector for East Tennessee by Gov. J.B. Frazier

June 15, 1903, a position he still holds and fills with efficiency and credit to himself.

Soon after his appointment, Mr. Tipton moved his family from Dunlap to this city where he now resides. After an experience of one year spent in visiting and inspecting the different mines of the state he is of opinion that Tennessee has the best mining law in America, and that both operators and workmen are evincing a determination to comply with its provisions which are intended for their mutual benefit.

ADVERTISEMENT FROM PAGE 13

Democratic Favorites

HON. A. A. ADAMS

Alfred Armstrong Adams, better known as Fred Adams, candidate for congress in the Fourth congressional district, of which Rhea county is a part, is a native of Wilson county having been born at Mt. Juliet April 9, 1865. His father was Alfred A. Adams, Sr., who served as a member of Buchannan's Co. "E," 1st Tenn. Cavalry, C.S.A., receiving wounds at Shiloh which afterward caused his death.

Fred Adams was reared upon a farm and when less than 15 years of age began life for himself; he succeeded in acquiring an education in the public schools, and graduated at Montgomery Bell Academy at Nashville, in June, 1885, with the highest honors of his class. He was the successful competitor for the orator's medal at Watkins Institute in Nashville in June 1885, having defeated some fifteen other competitors. In August of the same year, he won an appointment to a cadetship at West Point, New York, in a competitive examination at Hartsville, Tenn., in which contest some ten or twelve young men from the Fourth congressional district were competitors. He remained at the Academy until 1887 when he entered the Civil service of the government at Washington, D.C., and was assigned to duty in the office of the Auditor for the department, entering the service in the lowest grade and advancing by competitive examinations to the highest grade in the Civil Service. He was

HON· A A ADAMS

absolutely without means, and while working at his desk during the day, he made valuable use of his time by attending the night schools of the Washington Universities, completing his collegiate course, and graduating from both Georgetown and Columbia Universities, taking the degree of Master of Laws in the former; during his attendance of the Georgetown Law School the esteem in which he was held by class mates is attested by the fact that he was chosen president of his class consisting of over 100 bright young men from every state in the Union.

In 1897, he tendered his resignation and returned to his native county and begun the active practice of law at Lebanon, his present home. In 1900, he was elected from Wilson county to the State legislature. It was during this his first experience in legislative work that he demonstrated his ability as a law-maker. He immediately took front rank in that body and was identified with every measure looking to the moral and material welfare of the tax-payers of the state. He introduced and secured passage of the following measures:

1.   Prohibiting the sale of cigarettes in the state.

2.   Legalizing and regulating Primary elections.

3.   A law providing a method of assessing for advolorem taxes all railroad cars owned by corporations outside of the state but doing business in the state.

4.   Laws abolishing the taxing district of Lebanon, and a new charter for the town, thus applying the Four Mile Law.

5.   Providing a method by which towns operating under charters obtained under the general law may surrender their charters and reincorporate.

Besides these laws he secured the passage of several laws of a purely local nature. The following laws introduced by him passed the lower House:

1.   Abolishing the state board of equalization.

2.   Prohibiting sale of liquors on election days.

3.   Amending printing act requiring publication of public and private acts in separate volumes.

4.   Reducing appearance bonds from $250 to $100, in misdemeanor cases.

RECOMMENDED FOR PASSAGE

1.   To reduce to writing testimony in criminal cases before magistrates.

2.   Validating presentments signed only by foreman of grand jury.

3.   Giving blacksmiths a lien for work on vehicles.

The following amendments were proposed by him and adopted:

1.   To the road law requiring county courts to set apart not less than one-fourth of all money collected as privelege taxes for county purposes to be equally distributed among the road districts in each county. This amendment was contested by representatives from the cities. The farmers had for one hundred years borne the entire burden of road improvement and construction until this amendment was adopted. Mr. Adams is a warm advocate of all legislation tending to upbuild the county roads, and favors both state and national aid in road construction, believing that the farmer has burdens sufficient without having the whole burden of road improvement placed upon him alone. If elected to congress he stated in the first speech of his campaign that he would favor the bills pending in congress at the time of adjournment, looking to national aid in road construction.

2.   To the assessment law requiring county court clerks to turn over the tax books to the trustee on the first Monday in October instead of November, thus enabling them to go over the

counties and collect taxes saving the taxpayers the trouble of coming to the county seats to pay their taxes.

3. To the assessment law requiring the county boards of equalization to notify property owners before raising assessments.

He vigorously and effectively opposed the odious back tax attorney system.

He was a member of the sub-committee of the House which drafted the appropriation bill which cut down the expenditures of the state for the biennial term 1901-1902, over a quarter of a million dollars, reducing the per capita tax for state purposes to 87½, the lowest of any state in the Union.

So well did he serve his people that in 1903 he was elected to the state senate to represent Wilson and Smith counties. Here his ability as a legislator was recognized by the temperance element of the state who chose him to lead their fight for an extension of the Four Mile law on the floor of the senate. His ability as a ready debator, and accurate parlimentary leader is evidenced by his complete victory over the whiskey ring which has so long dominated the state and influenced its legislative policy.

While the delegation from Rhea county has been instructed for one of Mr. Adams' opponents, he has a large number of friends who hope that a contingency may arise whereby he may receive a division of the county's vote.

HON. M. G. BUTLER

Gen. M.G. Butler who is a leading candidate for congress before the democratic convention of the Fourth congressional district which assembles at Cookville July 14, was born in Jackson county, where he still resides, May 11, 1849. His father, Thos. H. Butler, held several positions of honor and responsibility, among them clerk of the circuit court, secretary of state and member of state senate. He also served as commissary in Stanton's 25th Tenn. regiment of the Confederate army from which he was discharged on account of inflammatory rheumatism.

HON. M. G. BUTLER.

The subject of this sketch was elected attorney-general of the 5th circuit in 1894 and served a full term, but declined a re-election on account of his wife's poor health. The 5th circuit is composed of the counties of Cumberland, Pickett, Putnam, Overton, Clay, Macon, Jackson, Smith, Trousdale and White. Gen. Butler has several times served as special judge, always having been elected by the bar for that purpose. This is a strong testimonial to his legal ability and the esteem in which he [is] held by his professional brethren.

The candidacy of Gen. Butler for congress has developed strong support [from] the delegations from Rhea, Cumberland, Morgan, Fentress and Jackson counties having been instructed to support him in the convention. He also has numberless friends in other counties of the district who are giving him hearty support and his followers are hoping, not without reason, for his triumphant nomination and election. And on account of his mature years and practical experience Gen. Butler's friends claim that in the event of his success, he will make one of the strongest members of the Tennessee delegation in the national house — a delegation that is exceptional for its strength, ability and influence.

HON. B. G. McKENZIE

Hon. B. G. McKenzie, Rhea county's choice for the state senate, was born in Meigs county, where he grew to manhood, thirty-eight years ago. He is a son of Esq. J.M. McKenzie and a member of the McKenzie family so well and so favorably known all over lower East Tennessee.

Having read law under Col. V.C. Allen, he established an office and began practice at Decatur about the year 1887. The following year he moved to this city where he has accumulated a competency and achieved distinction as a lawyer, devoting his attention mainly to the criminal courts in which he has a large business.

HON. B G M'KENZIE

Being a very pleasing, captivating stump speaker, Judge McKenzie has been much in demand in political campaigns. He has served in the capacities of city and county attorney, representative from Rhea county, and a number of times as special judge under the commission of the governor. But perhaps his most conspicuous public service was as representative in the legislature.

As a legislator, he especially distinguished himself. He introduced and secured the passage of a number of important measures among them one requiring corporations to redeem in cash the script or coupons issued to their working men. He it was who put through the now famous Rhea county redistricting act which has been the means of saving his constituents thousands of dollars in taxes. He was also a member of the joint committee which redistricted the state's judicial divisions effecting a great reduction in judicial salaries.

ADVERTISEMENT FROM PAGE 14.

As a man of force and influence Judge McKenzie is an easy superior to his opponents in the race. His rank if elected to the senate will not be a matter of conjecture. Rhea and Meigs counties have indorsed his candidacy and his prospects of receiving the nomination seem very promising.

HON. J. W. LILLARD

J. W. Lillard, or "Worth Lillard," as he is better known, was born at Decatur thirty-seven years ago and has lived all his life in Meigs county. He is a lawyer by profession (and a good one) having graduated from the law department of Cumberland University at Lebanon, Tennessee. His practice is confined for the most part to the chancery court in which tribunal he has a hand in nearly all of the litigation in his county.

Several positions of trust and responsibility have been filled by Mr. Lillard with ability and fidelity among them being clerk & master, post master at Decatur, commissioner of elections and county attorney. He now holds the latter position and has held it for many years. Though not an office-seeker, Mr. Lillard is well known to the political world. He has served as a member of the congressional committee, was nominated by his party in 1898 for joint representative for the counties of Meigs, James and Hamilton and though narrowly defeated, he swept his native county by an immense majority. Lately the democrats of Rhea and Meigs counties in their conventions have indorsed Mr. Lillard for representative. This action virtually makes him the party nominee and his election is practically assured.

From a recent letter to the editor of THE HERALD, we quote Mr. Lillard as follows:

"You can say for me as a candidate for the legislature, that if elected, I shall oppose any attempts to modify the four mile law, except to extend the territory covered by it; that all measures looking to the improvement of the free schools in the country districts will have my support; that as to local measures the majoirity of people affected should, and so far as my vote is concerned, shall control."

This indicates the character of the man whom the democrats have presented for legislative honors.

ADVERTISEMENT FROM PAGE 14

PAGE 15 OF ANNIVERSARY ISSUE

WE ARE GIVING FREE

WITH EVERY BOX OF

Japa-Cura Soap

A Pair of Scissors
Worth 40 Cents

REMEMBER You get THREE TEN CENT CAKES of Soap, and this pair of Scissors all for **25 CENTS**

We take especial pains with your Prescriptions and fill them at a live and let live price, and with the BEST DRUGS that money can buy.

We have on hand at all times a full line of the following, at prices that defy competition:

Drugs, Patent Medicines, Toilet Soaps, Perfumery Combs, Hair Brushes, Cloth Brushes, Tooth Brushes, Bath Brushes, Lather Brushes, Talcum Powders, in fact, everything usually kept in this line.

Also a nice line of Guaranteed Razors, Strops and Shaving Mugs

An immense line of STATIONERY of the Latest fads, including Tablets, Box and Bulk Papers. Our School Supply will be complete and we cordially invite the patrons of the Normal Institute to give us a call and get prices and examine our stock. We have a complete line of the celebrated Waterman and Parker Fountain Pens and can suit anyone in this line.

Gentlemen, don't forget that we carry the best line of CIGARS, SMOKING and CHEWING TOBACCOS and PIPES in this part of the country. We have gone down and dug up the mud sills of prices on Ball Bats, Mits, etc., and Croquet Sets, Fish Lines, etc.

We handle the full line of Medicines made by the BLACK HAW MEDICINE COMPANY and guarantee every package of these goods we sell. You positively run no risk whatever in trying these preparations. Asking a continuation of the patronage you have given J. T. Crawford in the past, and that you bring your friends to see us, We are your friends,

DAYTON DRUG CO.

Successors to J. T. CRAWFORD.

The Republican--Enterprise

VOL. XIII. NO. 3   DAYTON TENNESSEE FRIDAY AUGUST 30 1907   W. W. THELUS.

ONLY ONE MORE WEEK!
FOR OUR BIG BARGAINS

The Biggest and Best Selected Stock of
FALL AND WINTER GOODS
EVER SHOWN IN DAYTON
Is now arriving at our Store,

TO MAKE ROOM FOR THESE GOODS
We Must Dispose of Our Big Summer Stock
DURING NEXT WEEK

And we are Going to Treat the People of this
Section to the Most Extraordinary Bargains
EVER OFFERED IN DAYTON
FOR JUST ONE WEEK ONLY

THE DAYTON COAL & IRON COMPANY, Limited.
Dayton's Great Department Store.

FRONT PAGE OF 30 AUGUST 1907 ISSUE

74

ADVERTISEMENTS FROM PAGE 2 OF REPUBLICAN ENTERPRISE

THE REPUBLICAN-- ENTERPRISE
30 AUGUST 1907

Republican- Enterprise.

Weekly published in the best interests of Dayton and Rhea county.

W. W. SHIELDS, Editor & Pub.

Entered in at the Postoffice of Dayton Tenn. as second class mail matter.

Subscription 50cts per year in Advance

All communications for publication should reach this office, not later than Wednesday of each week; also the name of writer should accompany each ms. not for publication but as a guarantee of good faith.

Correspondence solicited.

[Page 1]

[NOTE: This page was covered with the Dayton Coal & Iron Company advertisement reproduced on page 73. B.J.B.]

[Page 2]

IN HONOR OF MISS GRACE CASH

Miss Alberta Long entertained fourteen guests Wednesday night at her home on Broyles street in honor of Miss Grace Cash.

Those present were: Misses Bell Sherman, Madge Rodgers, Lorena Cunnyngham, Blanch Pearcy, Grace Cash, Alberta Long, Sallie Cate Long; Messers Fred Purser, Fletcher Dodd, John Barton, Frank Purser, John Brewer, J. Johns, Carl Pearcy.

Refreshments were served at a late hour. The guests were all delighted with the evenings most enjoyable entertainment.

Dayton's Population Increased

K.M. Benson, clerk of the city school board, has just compiled the recent scholastic enumeration of the city. The work was performed by Mr. Benson, himself, and was carefully and thoroughly done.

The scholastic population of the city is as follows:

White—male 238, female 253, total 491.

Colored— male 102, female 111, total 213.

Total white and colored 704.

This is an increase of 32 over recent enumerations. The increase is due mainly to the fact that Mr. Benson's work was thorough and accurate.

On the basis adopted by statisticians and considered well nigh accurate, 5½ people to every school child, the population of Dayton is 4,026. This ratio is used as a basis in estimating the population of all the larger cities and there is no reason why it should not be as reliable in Dayton as elsewhere. It will be seen therefore that our population is at least double that given us by the census of 1900.

4,026 and still a growin'.

They are Coming Here

The best selection of clothing, furnishing goods, dry goods and notions to be found in this section is on display at J.R. Darwin's big store.

The new Kirschbaum hand made, high tailored suits are the highest class custon made suits on the market. The goods are of the highest quality. The weaves are of the latest design. The styles are the very latest out. They are all guaranteed to wear and retain their shape. There are no better or more fashionable goods on the market and you can get as perfect fit as any tailor can give you.

The fall shoes represents the most complete stock and best assortment ever carried by a Dayton house. Several of the most approved and up-to-date makes are carried in a variety of styles. We can fit any foot at almost any price.

Large consignments of all the late designs and patterns in dress goods are arriving daily. This stock was selected with great care and will be found strictly first class and up-to-date in every particular. A new lot of belts and combs have also arrived. In fact our fall stock in every line is complete from start to finish.

CARRIGAN'S SHAMPOO

A delightful hair dressing for ladies, children and gents. It kills the dandruff germ and is a sure cure for eczema. It is something swell for bathing the babies. For sale by both druggists — Crawford & Robinson and Thomison & Co. Manufactured by Albert J. Carrigan.

Why Patronize The Rhea County High School?

First — Because it is your school.

Second — Because it is more economical to you.

Third — Because its course of instruction is thorough and complete.

Fourth — Because its teachers are specialists in their line.

Fifth — Because you build up a home institution.

The high school belongs to the public. It belongs as much to the poorest, most insignificant man in Rhea county as it does to the richest, most influential. It is yours, whether you patronize it or not, and it cost you just as much if you fail to patronize it, as it costs if you do patronize it. It places a well grounded English education at your very doors. It opens the way for every boy and girl of Rhea county to obtain a first-class education. It is in its infancy and needs your influence and support. It is in your province to make it a power in the educational affairs of Rhea county. A first-class high school well maintained will place your county in the front rank among the other counties of the state. It will be an attractive proposition to home seekers from other states and sections.

Its cheapness should appeal to every parent. Tuition is absolutely free to all pupils of Rhea county, of whatever age. Light and fuel are furnished at actual cost. Table board furnished at the high school boarding hall, under the management of Prof. and Mrs. J.C. Fooshee, for 30 cents per day. Rooms in the dormitory free to girls. Boys can rent rooms very cheaply. No other educational institution can compete with the cheapness of the high school.

The course of study is as thorough and complete as is offered by any school of like character in the state. A thoroughly practical English education can be obtained here at home in this school. Those who seek a higher education are prepared for entrance to the colleges and universities where they will be admitted without further examination.

Each of the three teachers is a specialist in the branches coming under this supervision. Prof. J.C. Fooshee, principal, is a graduate of Terrell College and has taken special work on teaching in the University of Tennessee. Miss Mabel Fair, B.S., has had five years work in domestic science and history at the state university. Miss Daisy Wade, B.A., has had four years work in Latin and science at the state university. Few preparatory schools offer a stronger, better equipped faculty than our high school.

In the late examination for teachers 40 out of 65 failed to obtain certificates. It is a lamentable fact that a large percent of our teachers have to be imported from other counties. Simply because our own home boys and girls who desire to teach have heretofore been denied the facilities for the necessary preparation. Our school board and officials would gladly give preference to home teachers. The high school now offers adequate instruction to teachers and graduates are given teachers certificates without examination.

A library has been fitted up at the school building and 200 volumes of choice literature and standard works will be ready to use when school opens.

The building has been remodeled. The west room down stairs has been fitted up for use in the department of domestic science. A cooking and sewing room has been made.

The entire inside of the building has been overhauled and presents a new appearance.

Pupils are urged to wait until after the opening day to buy books.

The fall term will open on Monday morning at 10 o'clock when all pupils are urged to be present.

From Miss Kate Knight

Editor Enterprise:

Will you do me the very great favor to give to me sufficient space in the Enterprise to publish to the world a true, simple and unadorned story of the facts relating to my summary expulsion from membership in the First Baptist Church of Dayton and then allow an unprejudiced public to judge as to whether or not a great and unparalled wrong has been done to an innocent helpless girl.

I had been an humble member of the Baptist church from my childhood and I loved its associations and had implicit faith in its tenants. I had always tried hard to live a consistent Christian life and had in an humble way, freely given of both my time and limited means to promote the welfare of my church. No word of scandal had ever been uttered against my fair name until

sometime in March when "Evangelist" W.L. Head came to Dayton to hold a series of revival meetings. His coming was loudly heralded by the local press and extensively advertised by photo of the "Evangelist," conspicuously displayed in every show window, such as is used to announce the coming of a circus or menangerie.

Being an orphan, I have always made my home with my grandfather, R.C. Knight, whose house was ever a home to ministers of the gospel. The old gentleman offered the "Evangelist" the hospitality of his home and my grandmother, my sisters and myself waited on him like servants, for he was a minister of our faith, and we had always been taught to reverence all men of that calling.

And this "Evangelist" repaid our kindness and hospitality by grossly insulting the writer and later by joining in --?--laring slanderous reports detrimental to her character.

When grand-father approached him on the subject, he freely denied it with his lips, but loudly confessed his guilt by his actions in immediately packing his grip in an effort to silently steal away, which he would have done had he not been persuaded by a few of the "elect" of his fold to stand his ground and brazen it out.

A committee was appointed by the church to investigate the truth of the charge against the "Evangelist" composed of W.A. Howard, Whitlock and Rawlings, which committee reported without any evidence whatever having been taken and without giving me an opportunity to appear before it either in person or by counsil, that I was guilty of a great wrong in circulating such a report against a brother in the church and my pastor and recommending that I come before the church and apologize for so doing. The committee reported that the "Evangelist" was not guilty of the charge made against him by me, but that he was guilty of a very great wrong in violating the "Civil" law by unlawfully carrying a pistol.

The only evidence that was ever heard or considered by the committee, so far as I know, was my sworn statement that the "Evangelist" was guilty as charged and his denial which was not under oath. If any other evidence was heard or considered it was secretly given and such witness did not then, and does not now, dare to meet me face to face in the usual way of testifying. If such secret evidence was heard and considered I submit that it was cowardly in the committee and dastardly in the witness to then try to blast the character of an innocent girl in secrecy and darkness.

Having declined to apologize for telling the truth, I was summarily discharged from the church and my name dropped from the roll. One word as to the character of the so called "Evangelist" and I will leave a generous public to judge between us. My brother, Robert Knight, came home on a visit and learning of the insult offered me by the minister, he naturally resented it in his conversation with friends; thereupon, this "doughty" Evangelist, being advised thereto by one of the "elert," armed himself with a pistol and strutted the streets of Dayton with a deadly weapon in his pocket and dark murder in his heart. Having maligned the sister, he would murder the brother. But when he arrogantly and with a characteristic impudent swagger passed my brother on the street displaying the unmistakable outline of his pistol which he held barely concealed for instant use. My brother could not refrain from disarming him on the public street. It is correctly reported that the "Evangelist" on that memorable occasion displayed all the attributes of the "bully" and cursed and swore like a pirate.

But, however that may be, it is a matter of record that he was hauled before the July term of the Circuit Court when he took his proper place in the prisoners dock among negroes, outlaws and thugs and was fined $50.00 and costs for violating the criminal laws of the state instead of the divine law as the polite committee mildly states.

Such is the history and the character of the "Rev." W.L. Head and yet he is pastor of the First Baptist Church.

As my father and my father's father were both baptists as well as master masons and as two

of the committee were also master masons, I was quite confident that I would get a fair and impartial trial and would be permitted to meet the accusers face to face, but how sadly I was disappointed can be gathered from the facts herein related. From this great wrong done to my fair name I can only appeal to the judgment of a just and generous public, asking, begging, praying, it not to condemn me unheard, but to generously withhold its judgment until such time as I can be fully vindicated by the courts of the county and the law of the land. So vindictive is this "Evangelist" that he is now engaged in a desperate effort to excommunicate all those who differ with him in the least particular, or who express their sympathy for me and believe in my innocence. It is rank heresy to say a word detrimental to the swaggering parson.   KATE KNIGHT

Enterprise Ads Get Results

The value of The Enterprise as an advertising agency for quick results was demonstrated again last week. Miss Kate Cushing, the popular saleslady at J.R. Darwin's, lost a gold dollar pin. She advertised in these columns (as all wide-awake business people do for its return). The paper was issued Friday afternoon — Friday night Mrs. Rollings read the ad. She had found the pin and did not know the owner. Saturday morning she returned the pin to Miss Cushing who was very proud to regain her property.

Richmond Hosiery Mills

Few of our citizens are aware of the fact that the Richmond Hosiery Mills is providing an important factor in the financial affairs of Dayton.

Their fortnightly pay roll amounts to something over $200, and is distributed among those who would be unable to earn wages at any other work.

One young lady drew $16.25 Saturday for 12 days work— $4.00 more than the average man makes. Other young ladies and girls received from five and six to ten dollars for their work.

The money is deposited with the Dayton Bank & Trust Co. every two weeks to make their pay roll which is made out by Assistant Cashier B.B. Blevins without charge.

With the proper encouragement from our citizens this concern would soon branch out into one of our most important industries.

ADVERTISEMENTS FROM PAGE 2

ADVERTISEMENTS FROM PAGE 3

LOCAL PERSONAL

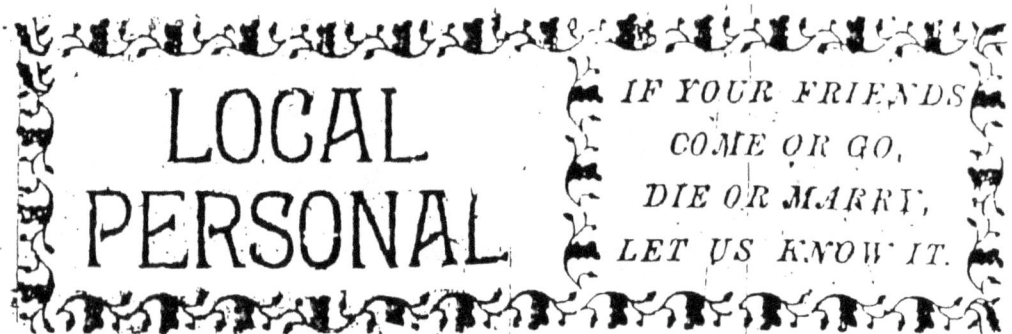

Carl Whitener and Edd Benson spent Sunday at Robbins.

Jackson Gross was in the city from Birchwood Saturday.

Miss Louella Abel, who has been of very invaluable service to her father, John Abel, in his mammoth store since school closed, is taking a week's vacation with relatives at Cleveland before school opens again.

Judge J.L. Godsey has been on the sick list for several days.

J.M. Maloney and niece, Miss Mary Shields, of Chattanooga, brother-in-law and daughter of W.W. Shields, were guests of his family in this city Sunday.

Large stock of first class Ready made skirts just received.   J.F. Henninger's

Trustee J.T. Crawford spent Sunday at Harriman on a visit to relatives. His son, Ayers, returned with him to Dayton.

F. Fisher was in the city from the old Seventh district Monday. Mr. Fisher is freely mentioned as the republican candidate for tax assessor at next election. Mr. Fisher, by reason of his long tenure as register, is familiar with land value throughout the county and is otherwise well equipped for this new county office.

E.P. Hutchins was down from Ogden Monday.

Ollie P. Darwin, representing the Spring City Mill Co., spent Monday in Dayton.

W.L. Douglass' shoes at J.F. Henninger's.

Squire J.D. Burkhalter and Rev. W.L. Head moved back to the city from the mountain Monday.

Rev. J.A. Whitener spent Sunday at Charleston.

Prof. Joe Benson was up from Chattanooga Sunday.

Misses Mae and Nannie Underwood, of Knoxville, spent the first of the week in Dayton as guests of the Misses Ault.

A substantial concrete sidewalk has been laid in front of the Methodist church of First Avenue.

Big lot of new school supplies, all kinds at Tomison's Drug Store.

Rev. H.S. Booth, the pastor, will begin a series of revival services at the Methodist church, South, Sunday morning. Mr. Booth is an earnest, devout minister, an able speaker and the services should be well attended.

See J.M. Hayes for seed rye.

School supplies of all kinds at Tomison's Drug Store.

J.R. Darwin and Will Robeson leave Tuesday for the Eastern markets, where they go to purchase the most select stock of Fall and Winter clothing, dry goods and furnishing goods ever put on display in this section.

Robert Mayer, of Chattanooga, was in Dayton Monday.

Ernest Henry spent Sunday at Bridgeport, Ala.

Thousands of Rhea County nubbins have been ruined by the recent rains.

Mrs. W.L. Head is visiting her parents in Atlanta, Ga.

B. Sykes was down from the mountain Tuesday.

Slippers are going at wholesale prices at J.F. Henninger's.

T.J. Watkins, of Birchwood, was in Dayton Tuesday.

Dr. W.W. Cunnyngham spent Tuesday in Chattanooga.

Mrs. W.O. Hudson was the guest of friends in Chattanooga Wednesday.

Judge M.S. Holloway was down from Spring City looking after county affairs Wednesday.

In order to avoid misunderstanding and controversy, citizens should notify Marshal W.J. Lowry of any street electric lights that fail to burn.

FOR SALE — A No. 1 pair of Young Mules, Wagon and Harness. Mules 4 years old and past. Wagon comparatively new. Will sell for cash or on credit. Apply to R.T. Howard, Dayton, Tenn.

Few people have any conception of the number of real estate transfers in Rhea county during a year. There have been 745 deeds recorded by Register W.A. Howard in the past 12 months. This is a rushing business for a county of Rhea's size.

Elder and Mrs. N.D. Reed and daughter, Mrs. John Gilbreath, spent Wednesday in Chattanooga.

Henry Jones was at home from Max Meadows, Va., greeting his numerous friends this week.

The Graysville base ball team defeated a crack Chattanooga team Saturday in a score of 5 to 4.

Mrs. D.B. Carlin is visiting relatives in Chattanooga.

Miss Susie Ault is spending several days in the Cincinnati and Louisville millinery emporiums studying the latest styles for fall and winter and selecting a choice line for her patrons.

Workhouse Commissioner A.J. Thompson, of Rhea Springs, one of the most practical members the workhouse commission has ever had, was in Dayton Thursday.

Rugs at Patton's.

Sam Nelson has been promoted [to] C. N.O. & T.N. Agent at Dayton and located at the South Dayton depot. R.P. Hodges succeeded Mr. Nelson as passenger agent at North Dayton. H.H. Taylor is in Cincinnati, and it is thought has been promoted to a better position. This news was received by wire this morning.

Editor D.M. Rhea, of the Rhea County News, was among the farmers at the Institute yesterday.

Ladies when in need of a pair of first class shoes see the new fall line of Dorothy Dodd Shoes at J.F. Henninger's.

Capt. John W. Morgan will be [a] candidate for re-election, office Secretary of State.

The biggest consignment of rugs ever received in Dayton are on display at the Dayton Furniture Co.

Every farmer in Rhea county should have been present at the Farmers meeting yesterday. Despite the fact that the meeting was held primarily to boast Judge Hull for reelection to congress, some most excellent addresses were made by representatives of the national and state department of agriculture. Judge Hull was on hand to tell the people how he would make the farms of the fourth district produce like the valley of the Nile if he were reelected. Mr. McFarland was here to tell us, if we wanted a real first-class farmer in Congress, where to find him.

Biggest assortment of trunks in Dayton. Patton has them at greatly reduced prices — Dayton Furniture Co.

Don't worry over that old stove when Patton is offering such rare bargains in Ranges.

A.J. Clark, the jeweler, leaves tomorrow for the eastern markets, where he will spend two weeks selecting the latest fads and fancies in jewelry and novelties.

Ola Smith, who has been very low of typhoid fever for several weeks, died Thursday. Out of more than fifty cases of typhoid in Dayton, this is the first to prove fatal.

Rugs, Rugs, in any quality or design, the most varied selection ever brought to Dayton — See Patton.

J.H. Pyott, of Dayton, came down yesterday for a visit to the city — Chattanooga News.

Mr. and Mrs. T.J. Pelfrey, of Clearwater, are down on a visit to their baby girl, Mrs. Tom King, in this city. Mr. Pelfrey is one of the old republican standby's of Rhea county.

Did you know that Mr. Charles Bruce, the popular Barber, who has been working in one of the best barber shops in Chattanooga, can be found at the Hotel Aqua Barber shop, where he and J.O. Wolf are always ready to wait on you? This is the only barber shop in the city that has hot and cold running water, tub and shower baths. Fred Stokes has full charge of the bath rooms. Clean towels to every customer. Give us a call once and you will certainly come back. My motto is "cleanliness and good work." Aqua Hotel Barber Shop, J.O. Wolf, Prop.

A.J. England, of Dayton, spent yesterday in the city — Chattanooga News.

Tablets, pencils and all kind of school supplies in great variety and abundance at Tomison's Drug Store.

Up to noon yesterday 94 men by actual count had attended the Hull rally at the court house. Now watch the Hull organs claim that thousands were present.

Best ranges on earth for the money — Patton at the Dayton Furniture Co.

J.A. Fee, one of the most popular and successful traveling men out of Cincinnati, is at the Stag, giving the glad hand to his numerous friends. He contemplates moving his family from Cincinnati to Dayton, Tenn., for the winter. His territory is in the south and Dayton. — Chattanooga News.

Marshal W.J. Lowery bought the fine John M. Howard strawberry farm yesterday for $1,500. This is one of the best paying small berry farms in Rhea county.

Those having business with banks will find the "Statement of the condition of the American National Bank" one of the most interesting items in this paper. This report shows the bank to be in a splendid condition. Its management is the most liberal to be found in a safe, conservative banking institution.

Col. W.L. Givens spent Wednesday at Decatur on professional business.

Miss Bertie Eaves, a former popular Dayton young lady, is up from Chattanooga visiting friends.

Reynold Sharp and Carl Patton leave Monday for Maryville to attend college.

John Barton, the clever little "soda jerker" at Crawford & Robinson's fountain, has returned from an extended vacation on the Cumberland Plateau.

Farmer Ben McKenzie, from the Stix, attended the Hull rally at the court house yesterday.

Dr. S.M. Yancy, of Washington, chaperoned his father, mother and sister, who have been his guests for several days, to Chickamauga Park Wednesday.

Miss Irene Johnson returned to her home in Chattanooga today after spending a fortnight in the city as a guest at Hotel Aqua.

Mrs. Euclid Waterhouse and Miss Mary Gillespie were shopping in Chattanooga Wednesday.

Miss May Johnson, of Chattanooga, is the guest of relatives and friends in the city.

Misses Daisy Wade and Mabel Fair, assistant teachers in the high school, arrived from Knoxville Wednesday.

Hon. John R. Neal was down from Rhea Springs to attend the Farmers Institute Thursday.

"Squire" Andy Grice treated several young ladies to a straw ride to New Union Tuesday night. Enroute the vehicle broke down and the "Squire" had to get another. If Andy hadn't been an acting "squire" the boys say, he could not have afforded so much expense.

James Crawford, of Dayton, spent Sunday [as] the guest of Mr. and Mrs. J.W. Ayers. Master Ayers Crawford, who has been spending the past two months with his grandparents, Mr.

and Mrs. J.W. Ayers, returned home with his father Sunday. — Harriman Observer.

Mrs. Tanksbury, of Harriman, stopped off for a visit with Mrs. J.E. Rankin Wednesday enroute home from Mont Eagle.

The "Home of New York" is one of the strongest, most reliable and prompt insurance companies in America. See Dodd & Givens.

Squire R.L. Marsh, of Birmingham, Ala., is on a visit to Dayton friends.

Mr. and Mrs. Will Purser, of Chattanooga, spent the first of the week in Dayton as guests of Mrs. Purser's mother, Mrs. Ault.

Col. V.C. Allen spent Tuesday in Chattanooga filing an inventory of the estate of Mrs. B.G. Pyott, deceased, of which he is executor.

Mr. and Mrs. B.C. Gardenhire, of Decatur, were in the city shopping Wednesday.

When you want fire insurance you want the safest and best. Let Dodd & Givens figure with you.

REPORT OF THE CONDITION OF THE AMERICAN NATIONAL BANK

---o---

At Dayton, in the State of Tennessee, at the close of business
Aug. 22, 1907

---o---

RESOURCES

Loans and Discounts	$ 115,816.97
Overdrafts, secured and unsecured	981.76
U.S. Bonds to secure Circulation	7,000.00
Bonds, securities, etc.	16,978.65
Banking house, furniture & fixtures	5,800.00
Due from National Banks (not reserve agents)	46,275.02
Due from approved reserve agents	19,821.23
Checks and other cash items	176.18
Notes of other National Banks	1,000.00
Fractional paper currency, nickles and cents	228.64

LAWFUL MONEY RESERVE
IN BANK, VIZ:

Specie	9,524.60	
Legal tender notes	4,385.00	13,859.60
Redemption fund with U.S. Treasurer (5% of circulation)		350.00
TOTAL		$ 227,990.47

LIABILITIES

Capital stock paid in	$ 25,000.00
Surplus fund	20,500.00
Undivided profits, less expenses and taxes paid	1,566.00
National Bank notes outstanding	7,000.00
Individual deposits subject to check	104,248.77
Demand certificates of deposit	69,067.15
Cashier's checks outstanding	607.95
TOTAL	$ 227,990.17

STATE OF TENNESSEE,
COUNTY OF RHEA:

I, W.B. Allen, Cashier of the above-named bank, do solemnly swear that the above statement is true to the best of my knowledge and belief.　　　W. B. ALLEN, Cashier

Subscribed and sworn to before me this 27th day of Aug., 1907.

P.T. FOUST, Notary Public
CORRECT — ATTEST
A. P. HAGGARD
W. H. ROGERS　　　　　　Directors
J. H. ROGERS

Teacher's Program

First monthly meeting of the Rhea County Teachers Association for the scholastic year 1907-1908, to be held at the court house Saturday, Sept. 7, 1907.

9:00 — Invocation.

9:15 — Loyalty to our school system, W.E. Stephens.

9:45— Number work in primary grades, Miss Myrtle Boyd.

10:15 — Added duties and responsibilities, Fred B. Frazier.

10.45 — How shall we improve our institute's work this year, J.C. Fooshee.

11:15 — Roll Call.

11:30 — Noon Recess.

1:00 — The proper grading of our schools and the advantages of recitations at desks, Walter White.

1:30 — Importance of Domestic Science in School work, Miss Mabel Fair.

2:00 — Organization and Miscellaneous business.

COMMITTEE

ENJOYABLE BALL

The ball given at the opera house last evening by the Dayton Social Club was one of the most enjoyable events ever given in this city.

Dancing was indulged in till a late hour when the party proceeded to Crawford & Robinson's Ice Cream Parlor where delicious refreshments were served.

Out of town participants were: Misses Irene Johnson, Chattanooga; Stella McDonald, Harriman; Francis and Louis Spurlock, Rhea Springs; Susie Saul, Atlanta, Ga.; ---- [sic] Murphy, Butte, Mont.; Mrs. Bertie Bowling, Chattanooga; Mrs. Spurlock, Rhea Springs.

Mr. and Mrs. B.C. Gardenhire, Decatur.

Messrs. Charles Howard, Chattanooga; Cyrus Darwin, Evensville; Roy Williams, Rhea Springs; Henry Knox, Chattanooga.

Street Work Needed

The attention of the street committee is called to the condition of Maine street, between Market and the passenger depot.

This is one of the most public and most important streets in the city and just a little work will make it one of the best.

There is more travel over this street than over any other in Dayton. Some of the most valuable business property in Dayton is on this part of the street and more business is done here than on other streets of the same length in Dayton.

The street has a solid substantial bed but the top dressing has washed off leaving rough stones sticking up and ruining what with but little work would be the best street in Dayton. We are sure that if the committee will examine the street the needed repairs will be made at once.

ADVERTISEMENT FROM PAGE 3

ADVERTISEMENTS FROM PAGE 3

[Page 4]

CARNIVAL OF CRIME

Last Friday evening, near Morgantown, John and Fred Stansberry and Charley Nixon became involved in a difficulty with Jim Campbell, colored, in which Campbell was severely stabbed. It is reported that the trouble arose over a crap game and that Campbell had one of the Stansberry boys down when Nixon did the stabbing. The parties have all been arrested.

Sunday, about noon, Whit Green and Horace Dillard became involved in a difficulty near the coke ovens and Horace cut and slashed his brother Green and uncle Whit almost fatally. He has so far eluded the officers.

Too much bad liquor is said to be responsible for both difficulties.

Saturday night the South Dayton depot was broken into and the safe badly battered. Nothing, so far as known, was taken. This is the second time within two weeks that the depot was entered.

Mrs. Pyott's Estate

Judge V.C. Allen, executor of the estate of the late Mrs. B.G. Pyott, yesterday filed an inventory of the estate together with a report of the board of appraisers appointed to value real estate left to the various heirs by the will of Mrs. Pyott. This board consisted of A.F. Armstrong, W.B. Zeigler, John Zeigler and T.J. Robinson, the real estate being situated in Hamilton and Rhea counties.

The statement disclosed receipts of cash, income from rental property, certificates of deposit and other cash items to the amount of

$14,906.97, with disbursements to heirs, and expenses incidental to winding up the estate $14,487.18, leaving a cash balance on hand of $469.79.

The statement submitted by the appraisers of the value of the real estate to the various heirs is as follows:

Two tracts of land willed to James H. Pyott, $9,000.

Three tracts of land willed to John E. Pyott, $16,000.

Two tracts of land willed to Charles P. Pyott, $14,000.

The Garrison farm willed to Annie Pyott, $15,000.

Two tracts of land willed to Cora N. Pyott, $11,500.

Two tracts of land and two islands in the Tennessee river, $18,500.

Mrs. Pyott died some time ago and was a resident of Chattanooga for a number of years. Most of the property left consisted of farm lands. — Chattanooga Times.

Waterson At His Best

---o---

Plea Against Hypocrisy
And For His Old Kentucky

I protest against that religion which sands the sugar and waters the milk before it goes to its prayers. I protest against that morality which poses as a saint in --?--blie [blank spot on page] to do as it pleases in private. As the old woman said of the old man's swearing, "If there's anything I do hymeninate it is hypocrisy," In my opinion that which threatens Kentucky are not the gentlemanly vices of the race course and the sideboard, but perfidy and phariseeism in public and in private life.

The men who made the Bluegrass famous, who put the brand of glory upon its women, its horses and its vintage, were not ashamed to take a drink nor to lay a wager though they paid their losses and understood where to draw the line. They marked the distinction between moderation and intemperance. They did not need to be told what honor is. They believed, as I believe, that there is such a thing as pretending to more virtue than honest morals can hope to attain.

I refuse to yield to these. Holding the ministry in reverence, as spiritual advisors, rejecting them as emissaries of temporal power, I do not intend, if I can help it, to be compelled to accept a rule of modern clericalism which, if it could have its bent and sway, would revive for us the pios-ridden systems of the middle ages. I do not care to live in a world that is too good to be genial; too ascetic to be honest, too proscriptice to be happy. I do not believe that men can be legislated into angels — even red-nosed angels.

When the time arrives for me to go to account, I mean to go shouting; to go with my flag flying; and, as I never have lied to the people of Kentucky, please God, I never shall. I have told them a great many unpalatable things. I have met their disapproval full in the face. I have lived to see most of my admonitions against this, that and the other vain hope, vindicated by events. I want to live yet a little longer still to tell the truth and shame the devil; but if ol--?--nrity and adversity and neglect shall overtake me it will be a comfort even in the valley of the shadow of death that from first to last I fought, not for the speaked gospels of the shorthaired woman and the long-haired men of old Babylon, but for the simple mannered and lovely womanhood of old Kentucky — never New Kentucky, but always and forever Old Kentucky — your birthright and mine.

Resolution of Respect

NOLA WALKER

God has borne from our Junion League our dear little Nola Walker. It was hard to part with our darling, but God's wisdon is greater than ours! This dear little flower is not dead, she is just blooming in a heavenly home. She was one of our dearest members that we loved and were so sad to have her taken from us, but she has gone to her home in heaven. We long to meet her and we know that she will welcome us home.

She took the typhoid fever and was sick only a few days, until God thought best to take her home to rest.

Nola called her parents and sisters to her bed-side and told them to meet her in heaven. May God help them to meet their sweet children. She bore her pains and sufferings so patiently.

Our dear little Nola has gone to her home beyond the sky leaving many friends behind to mourn her absence.

God help the bereaved family to bear their sorrow until they meet again.

JESSIE HEAD
MYRTLE HENDERSON
IVA RIGSBY   Committee

"EVERYBODY SHOULD KNOW" says G.G. Hays, a prominent business man of Bluff, Mo., that Bucklen's Arnica Salve is the quickest and surest healing salve ever applied to a sore, burn or wound, or to a case of pri--?--. I've used it and know what I'm talking about. Guaranteed by Crawford & Robinson, Druggist. 25¢

Unclaimed County Warrants

County warrants remain in the county court clerk's office unclaimed as follows:

NAME	DATE	AMT.
H.M. McElwee	Dec 18, 1905	$ 1.00
J.S. Foust	"	1.00
J.H. Pearson	"	1.00
W.R. Grimsley	"	1.00
J.W. Kyle	"	1.00
Tom Rogers	Feb. 9, 1906	1.00
H. Morgan	Mch. 16, 1906	1.00
J.O. Benson	Mch. 11, 1906	5.30
W.E. Wilkerson	"	1.00
W.S. Tallent	"	1.00
E.D. Pearce	"	1.00
E.M. Crosby	"	1.00

S.B. Ballard	Mch. 11, 1906	$ 1.00
H.C. Devault	Aug. 7, 1906	1.00
J.A. Swinford	"	.25
R.M. Sherman	Oct. 2, 1906	1.00
J.C. Abernathy	"	.50
J.T. Darwin	"	.50
W.J. Jolly	Nov. 13, 1906	1.00
F.H. Ingle	"	1.00
H.M. McElwee	"	1.00
Q.A. Tallent	"	1.00
R.L. Wilkey	"	1.00
J.W. Gillespie	"	1.00
J.C. Morgan	"	1.00
J.M.B. Headlee	"	1.00
A. Kaylor	Jan. 10, 1907	.50
Oas Goins	Feb. 14, 1907	.50
H.D. Webb	Mch. 14, 1907	2.00

CITY OF DAYTON

Mayor	James Miller
City Attorney	J.B. Swafford
Clerk and Recorder	J.L. Godsey
Treasurer	B.B. Blevins
Marshall	W.J. Lowery

Alderman, 1st Ward — Joe Morgan, Jas. Miller
2nd Ward — E.P. Johnson, J.L. Daniel
3rd Ward — Arch Rollins, N.J. Tallent
4th Ward — C.D. Sanborn, W.M. Brown

RHEA COUNTY

Chairman County Court	M.S. Holloway
Clerk, County Court	W.B. Kelly
County Attorney	J.B. Swafford
Sheriff	J.H. Frazier
Trustee	J.T. Crawford
Circuit Court Clerk	W.B. Allen
Clerk & Master	T.J. Gillespie
Coroner	R.C. Knight
Supt. of Education	Fred B. Frazier
Register	W.A. Howard
Election Commissioners:	E.F. Waterhouse,
	J.L. McKenzie,
	J.M. Hayes

Rhea County High School

BEGINS SEPTEMBER 23, CLOSES MAY 1, 1908 — 8½ MONTHS

Enrollment in High School proper 94. Four years courses in History, Mathematics, English, Latin and Sciences. Two Years course in Domestic Science. Special Training for Teachers. Graduates licensed to teach in Rhea County without examination; also admitted to the University of Tennessee. This is the connecting link between the rural schools and the State University. Library and Physics laboratory recently added. Tuition free to all students in Rhea County. Rooms in boarding hall free for girls. Table board at boarding hall 30 cents a day, or $ 2.10 a full week of seven days. Room cheap for those wishing to do their own cooking. Tuition for those outside of Rhea County $2.00 to $2.50. Music teacher in school building.

Courses of study and full particulars upon request.

J.C. FOOSHEE, Principal   Dayton, Tennessee

ADVERTISEMENTS FROM PAGE 4

91

ADVERTISEMENTS FROM PAGE 4

THE WEEKLY HERALD
13 SEPTEMBER 1907

The Colored Herald

ISSUED EVERY FRIDAY

T. J. CAMPBELL

EDITOR AND BUSINESS MANAGER

OFFICE: Hudson Block Up-Stairs

Entered at the Post Office at Dayton, Tennessee, as second-class matter for transmission through the mails.

DOMESTIC SCIENCE

And Its Importance in Connection With School Work

[Paper read before the Teacher's Institure here last Saturday by Miss Mabel Fair]

Will you pardon me if I change the subject just a little and call it the "Importance of Home Economics" in the school, because "Home Economics" comes nearer explaining what we mean by the work than does "Domestic Science."

They say we go to school to get an education; if this is so, we must determine what education is. Educators agree that a truly educated person is at home in any condition, or any place he may find himself — that education is to fit or prepare to live.

Now to live and live lightly, we must be mentally and physically well. Pope, in his "Essay on Man," says: "Reason's whose pleasure, all the joys of sense lies in three words — health, peace and competence." People who are not healthy cannot make competent citizens.

Let us see just what sickness costs America today. On an average every American is on the sick list for nine days in each year. If we take the population of the U.S. as 80,000,000, that makes almost two million years of sickness every year. Industrially 2,000,000 years of human life anually go to waste, and moreover, the sufferers demand a great deal of time and effort from those who are well.

Just one invalid seems insignificant, but think how many there are in the world or even in a community. Count up the lost days of usefulness and the total indicates enormous cost; a pitful waste, a mighty problem.

Dr. P.M. Hall estimated that the loss of wages at an average of $1.00 per day to every invalid would amount to more than $700,000,000 per annum. Cost of treatment will easily amount to as much again. This sickneess costs the U.S. something like one and one-half millions annually, a sum not greatly below the combined value of our two greatest manufacturing industries, of iron and steel and textiles.

Thus we see sicknerss is a sin, because waste is sin and God has given us our lives we should make the best of them. We all then, should learn to be healthy, happy, efficient human beings. In our school curriculums we have placed sciences. Why is this? You immediately answer, it is to teach the students the laws of nature — the laws that govern falling bodies, the laws of force and energy. Are we not a part of nature too? If so, we are subject to her laws. Is it more important to know the amount of coal it takes to run an engine than it is to know the amount of air, water and food that is necessary to keep those living machines of ours, these bodies,

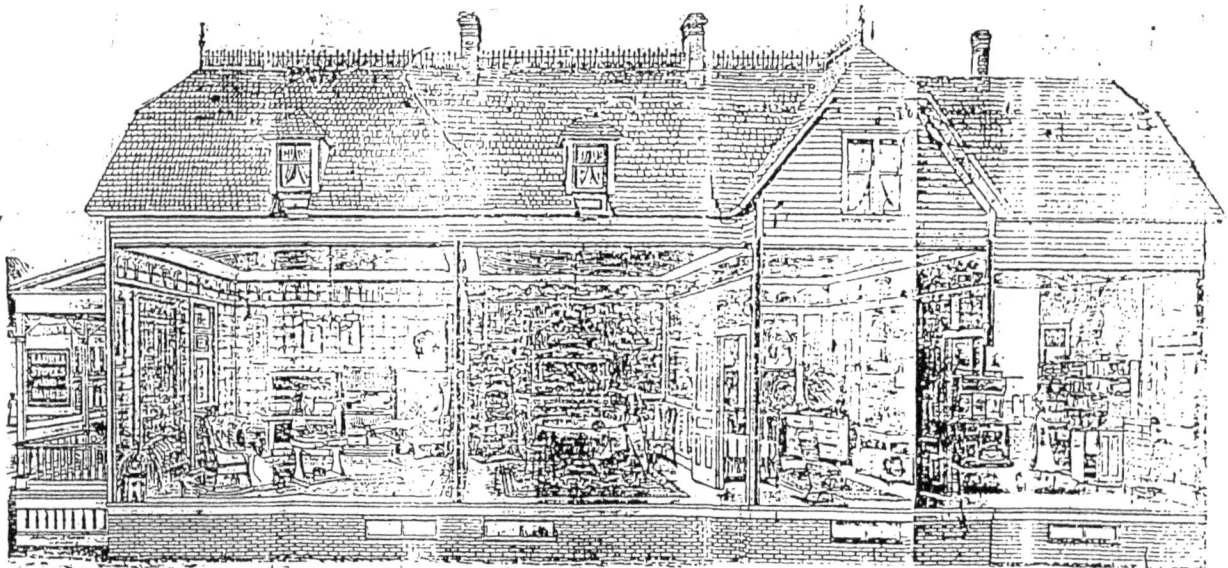

ADVERTISEMENT ON LOWER HALF OF FIRST PAGE

in such a condition that they will enable us to do the best work?

Home Economics deals with the problems of right living, and as we said before a strong, healthy body is essential to efficient citizenship and for good care of the body we must have fresh air, pure water, good wholesome food, carefully prepared, cleanliness in all things, exercise, amusement, sleep and mental environment in so far as we can control our surroundings. Each one of these subjects is a problem in itself and a very important one; but the subject at hand is the most important. When we realize that the --?-- loss or improper feeding of a little child for just one day may cause him to be a dyspeptic all his life, it impresses me with its importance.

Food, housing (including heat and light) and clothing, are absolutely necessary, and Dr. Engle, who has given this problem special attention, has worked out the proportionate expenditures as follows — and given us what is known as the Four Laws of Engle:

1st Law is that the proportion between expenditure and nutriment grow in geometrical progression in an inverse ratio to well-being. In other words the higher the income the smaller the percentage of cost of subsistence.

2nd. Is that clothing assumes and keeps a distinctly contrast proportion in the whole.

3rd. Is that lodging, warming and lighting have an inviable proportion whatever the income.

4th. Is that the more the income increases the greater is the proportion of different expenses, which expenss the degree of well-being.

Therefore, the less a worker gains the more he invests in food, renouncing out of necessity all other desires. Then to get the best out of the amount we have to spend we must consider the nutriment of the food, and find out what food is cheap and why. In this day one can live on ten cents a day if he only knew how and is not more than ninety miles from a railroad. But it takes a $5,000 wife to live on a $500 income. Why not make all our girls equal to or greater that a

$5,000 value by giving them a thorough course in Home Economics.

Home Economics used to be taught in the home, but today you find that neglect to quite an extent, and our women are becoming wage earners; especially the married women. They would rather work in a store or uptown office than tend to their own homes and children; there is something wrong, probably they consider housekeeping and home life drudgery. And why do they consider it so? Simply because they do not know the importance of it. They cannot see future results, only the present gratification and pride.

In Home Economics we hope to teach the girls to be more efficient women and better mothers for our future children.

I leave to you to decide the importance of such work in our public schools.

[Page 2]

"YOU ALL" IN THE SOUTH
---o---
What Makes This Popular Phrase A Provincialism

Philologists claim that some of the most interesting phases of a language may be traced through the medium of so called colloquialisms and idioms, and a consideration of the phrase "you all," as used throughout the south, would certainly seem to make good this assertion. The subject is treated in Uncle Remus' Magazine in an article by C. Alphonso Smith of the University of North Carolina. He says in part:

"In almost every discussion of this idiom the disputants have confined themselves to the question, 'Is it used in the south as a singular?' Northern writers have generally supported the affirmative, while southern writers have defended the negative. In fact, Mason and Dixon's line will have to be retraced and made to mark not a political but an idiomatic distinction. The shibboleth is no longer. What do you think of slavery or secession or states rights? but, On the contested use of you all are you for the singular or for the plural?

"Southern people undoubtedly use you all in a sense particularly their own and not as the equivalent of all of you.

"What, then, is the distinctive meaning attached to this idiom in the south? What makes the phrase a provincialism as used in the south, but not a provincialism as used elsewhere? The following sentences will illustrate:

"First. — A mother to her children, 'If you all (you children) don't make less noise, I'll send you to bed.'

"Second. — A teacher to his pupils, 'You all (you pupils) haven't half studied this lesson.'

"In not one of these characteristic sentences would a southerner ever think of substituting all of you for you all. Both idioms are plural, but the distinctive thing about southern you all is not its plural sense, but its representative sense, together with the accent on you.

"You all, therefore, with the accent on you, is not an error for you all, with the accent on all, or for all of you.

"It is something entirely different. The standard you all and all of you are employed as frequently in the south as elsewhere, the distinctive you all supplying a desideratum not furnished by either of the other two phrases. Joel Chandler Harris writes as follows:

" 'You may say without any hesitation whatever that "you all" and "we all," "you uns," "we uns," invariably refer to more than one individual. These locutions sometimes refer to a partner, to a family, to a settlement and to a whole community, but never to one individual. I have seen assertions to the contrary, but you may put them down as gross mistakes.' "

A Noble Critic

When Pope was first introduced to Lord Halifax to read his "Iliad," the noble critic generously critizised this passage and that word at frequent intervals. The poet was stung with vexation, for the parts that most pleased him were the ones most critized. As he returned home with Sir Samuel Garth, he revealed his displeasure:

"Oh," said Garth, "you are not acquainted with his lordship. He must criticize. At the next visit read him the same passage, and tell him you recollected his criticisms." Pope made use of this strategem. Lord Halifax was delighted and exclaimed, "Pope, they are now inimitable."

Faced the Lions

African Explorer (spinning a yarn) — Not very long ago I went out one day unarmed, when I suddenly found myself face to face with three lions.

Friend — Well?

Explorer — I fixed my gaze on the brutes, then stuck my hands in my pockets and walked away, whistling an air from an opera.

Friend — And didn't the lions immediately rush at you?

Explorer — They couldn't. It was at the zoo — London Tid-Bits.

Apple Trees on Wet Land

It is generally known that apple trees are very impatient of wet feet. This can easily be seen in orchards where there are small spots of poorly drained land where the water stands, remarks Country Gentleman. In such spots the trees are always poor, and they usually die out early, leaving these places blank in the orchard. It has been observed that a twisted growth of the apple tree trunk indicates imperfect underdrainage.

THE SOUTH AND THE RAILROADS

It might be well enough for Atlanta to drive the Southern Railway out of the transportation business within the limits of that state, so that the people may realize what a grand and glorious thing it is to have no railroads to grind them to the earth. It seems to be the determination of Alabama to test the thing and make a serpentless Eden by turning the state into a railroadless Alabama.

There are in this country 250,000 miles of railroad, operated by corporations that any one of 10,000 politicians will tell you hold all the 80,000,000 and odd of us to a condition of peonage. Alabama and Arkansas too, likewise North Carolina, are weary of the thing and have taken steps to make it unprofitable to operate railroads within their limits. This the day of justice is but a little way ahead and the yoke of the railroads will be lifted.

The Post is not lawyer enough to say whether a state has the right to nulify any clause of Section 2, Article III, of the Constitution of the United States by indirection. The law of Alabama requires a foreign corporation to abdicate its right under the constitution before it can be licensed to operate a railroad in that state. This is meat for the Supreme Court, and the sooner that tribunal sits down to it the better for Alabama and the railroads.

If the railroad mileage of Alabama were double what it is, the transportation facilities of that state would not be equal to those enjoyed by the people of Indiana. No state is more abundantly endowed by nature than Alabama. Soil and climate are all that could be desired. Her mountains and hills are full of iron, coal and stone. Birmingham is one of the marvels of American energy and the product of railroads. The northern part of the state should abound in manufacturing cities aggragating millions of inhabitants, busy in the lives of industry. All that is lacking is for the corporations and the people to practice justice in their mutual intercourse and be friends.

And friends they would be if it were as odious for politicians to practice demogogy in Alabama as it now is for corporations to operate railroads in that state. No other section is so sorely in need of more and better roads as the South. It is a blind, fatuous folly for the South to discourage the railroad business, but that is what the South is doing, and at a time when that region was never so prosperous and its destiny never so promising. — From The Washington Post, Washington, D.C., August 10, 1907.

There are a great many people who have slight attacks of indigestion and dyspepsia nearly all the time. Their food may satisfy the appetite but it fails to nourish the body simply because the stomach is not in fit condition to do the work it is supposed to do. It can't digest the food you eat. The stomach should be given help. You ought to take something that will do the work your stomach can't do. Kedel For Indigestion and Dyspepsia, a combination of natural digestants and vegetable acids, digests the food itself and gives strength and health to the stomach. Pleasant to take. Sold by Crawford & Robinson and W.F. Thomison.

As Good As She Sent

Years ago the once famous Mr. and Mrs. Barney Williams were playing an engagement at the Boston museum. The couple were always great favorites in Boston, but Mrs. Williams was somewhat noted for her sharp tongue both on and off the stage.

On the night in question she had been disturbed by the crying of a baby in the gallery. Stepping to the footlights, she stopped in the middle of her lines and, looking toward the offending child, cried, "Wanted, a nurse!"

To this came in a rich brogue from the child's mother, so that all the house heard, "No Irish need apply." — Boston Herald.

98

The Pitman and the Owl

A pitman, when coming through a plantation not far from Barnsley, found an owl, almost dead. Picking it up, he thought he might pull it round if he kept it warm, so, taking this mother's shawl, for she was in bed and knew nothing of the proceedings, he wrapped up the poor bird and placed it beside the fire. Next morning, on his mother's arrival in the kitchen, she saw the owl perched on the hob. She exclaimed, "Why, I always thought our George was a clever lad; blessed if he hasn't gone and stuck a neb on the cat?" — Dundee Advertiser.

There Were Others

"Am I the only girl you ever loved?"

"Oh, no!" he answered promptly, "You are the sixth."

"The sixth!" she exclaimed, suddenly relieving his shoulder of the weight of her head.

"Yes," he said coldly, "there were five before you — my mother, an aunt and three sisters."

And thereafter she endeavored to be more specific when she asked questions.

ADVERTISEMENTS FROM PAGE 2

ADVERTISEMENTS FROM PAGE 2

[Page 3]

DIRECTORIES

OFFICIAL — COUNTY

CHANCERY COURT convenes at Dayton semi-annually, the First Monday in February and August. T.M. McConnell, Chancellor; T.J. Gillespie, Clerk & Master.

CIRCUIT COURT sits at Dayton Tuesdays after the second Mondays of March, July and December. Joseph C. Higgins, Judge; W.B. Allen, Clerk.

COUNTY COURT meets in Quarterly session First Mondays in January, April, July and October. M.S. Holloway, Chairman; W.B. Kelley, Clerk. Members: First District, C.J. Russell, W.D. Smith; Second District, J.F. Leuty, J.L. DeVaney, M.S. Holloway, W.P. McDonald; Third District, J.D. Burkhalter, Martin Wilkey, S.F. Knight; Fourth District, R.H. Barger, J.W. Truex; City of Dayton, Alex Green, A.N. Grice.

Sheriff —	Jas. S. Frazier
Trustee —	J.T. Crawford
Register —	W.A. Howard
Supt. of Schools —	Fred B. Frazier
Surveyor —	J.L. Daniel
County Attorney —	J.B. Swafford
Election Commissioners — J.A. Torbet, E.F. Waterhouse, J.M Hayes	

OFFICIAL — CITY

The Board of Mayor and Alderman meets monthly, the First Monday evening of each month. The following compose the government.

Mayor —	R.M. Sherman
Recorder —	J.L. Godsey
Marshal —	W.J. Lowry
Treasurer —	B.B. Blevins
Supt. of Schools —	S.N. Varnell

Board of Aldermen — J.L. Miller, J.C. Morgan, J.L. Daniel, E.P. Johnson, A.H. Rollings, N.J. Tallent, C.D. Sanborn, W.M. Brown.

Board of Education — Alex Green, H.H. Taylor, F.H. Abel, K.M. Benson, J.F. Henninger, W.C. Bailey.

CHURCH AND FRATERNAL

M.E. CHURCH — Services every Sunday at 10:45 a.m., W.C. Haltom, P.C., Sunday School at 9:30, C.D. Sanborn, Supt. Epworth League 3:00 p.m., Fred Denton, Pres.

M.E. CHURCH, SOUTH — Services at 11 a.m. and 7:30 p.m. each Sunday. Sunday School at 9:30. Rev. H.S. Booth, P.C.; W.A. Ault, Supt.

FIRST BAPTIST — Services Sundays at 11 a.m. and 7:30 p.m. Rev. W.L. Head, pastor. Sunday school 9:30 a.m., Wm. Whitlock, Supt.

SECOND BAPTIST — Services on Sundays at 10:30 a.m. and 7:30 p.m., also Saturdays at 7:30 p.m. Sunday school 9:30 a.m. A. Brumagin, Pastor.

CHRISTIAN CHURCH — Preaching at Presbyterian Church Second Sunday of each month at 11 o'clock by Dr. E.H. Boyd. Sunday school each Lord's Day at 10 a.m., J.L. Daniel, Supt.

ODD FELLOWS — Dayton Lodge No. 2, I.O.O.F., meets every Tuesday evening. W.A. Dodd, N.G.; Taylor Brandon, V.G.; F.A. Reed, Secretary.

KNIGHTS OF PYTHIAS — Hope Lodge No. 57, Knights of Pythias, meets every Friday evening. L.E. Cunnyngham, C.C.; W.B. Allen, K.R.S.

F. & A.M. — Dayton Lodge No. 512 meets first Monday evening in each month. A.J. Holden, W.M.; W.L. Lillard, Sec.

[Only the first paragraph of the following article on Packing Vegetables was type-copied. The banner heading and illustration is also reproduced. B.J.B.]

Farm, Field and Garden

PACKING VEGETABLES
Some Kinds of Truck Shipped in the Barrel Basket

Cucumbers are shipped in the open third barrel veneer baskets. The cut shows a basket ready for heading up. The cucumbers, as will be seen, are not placed in the basket indistcriminately, but are arranged by hand so as to fit closely and to leave a flat surface on top for the placing of a cover. . . .

BASKET OF CUCUMBERS

A Cool Dairy Without Ice

An ingenious woman has devised a plan for having good, cool milk and butter all summer without ice. It is a homemade dairy, is cheap and easily taken care of and is successful. I will give the plan, and any housewife can have it made with very little work, says H.E.K. in American Cultivator.

Get four pieces of scantling 2 by 4 inches, six feet long, and nail pieces two feet long each way about two and a half feet from the ground and nail pieces of the same at the top. Then board over top and also lay a floor at the bottom. Now put a shelf in each side and cover all around and on top with nice clean bran sacks or burlap. Leave one side open and put loops on it and nails on the side to fasten it.

Put a tub on top and fill it with water and put woolen strips of cloth two or three inches wide in it so that they feed the water down, and keep the sacking wet all the time. The air blowing through the wet sacks keeps everything almost as cool as if it were in a refrigerator and the butter and milk taste better than if they were shut from the air and will keep fresh much longer in this dairy. An old blanket makes the best feeding strips. Put in enough to have three or four to each side.

This dairy was kept in the yard under a shade tree, but a cool back porch is equally as good a place and more convenient. Any one who tries this plan I am sure will be delighted with it.

Rehearsal in a Car

"The other night, coming home in the car," said the professional entertainer, "I began to wonder if I could bring tears to my own eyes as I do to the eyes of the other people. I tried. I thought of all the wrongs I had committed and felt sorry for people I had wronged. I though of all the mistakes I had made that other people had profited by, and pretty soon the tears began to gather in my eyes and roll down my cheeks.

"I forgot there were other people in the car who might notice me. Soon a woman got up from across the car and came to me.

" 'I see, sir,' she said, 'that you are in some trouble. Can I do anything to help you?'

"Lord bless you, no madam," I told her, hastily wiping away my tears. "I am a professional entertainer and was practicing on myself. That's all." — New York Press.

WOMEN OF HOLLAND

Their Costumes Too Complex For Words, Says a Feminine Writer

The women's costume is a trifle too complex for verbal description, as feminine belongings usually are, says Florence Craig Albrecht in Scribner's, but the white lace cap which covers the head from over brows to nape of neck and from ear to ear, curving out in rounded wings on each side of her cheek, is always a conspicuous and inevitable portion of a woman's attire. It may possibly be that on Sunday the cap is a trifle whiter or stiffer or daintier than on week days, but the difference is not very apparent.

The ladies assure us that there is vast difference in the quality of the net and the amount of handiwork employed, but the lens made no special note of that. In shape and outline the camera finds great distinction between these caps and those of Katwyk or Marken or Bois le Duc, but between Sunday and Monday caps in Volendam it records none whatever.

For the rest of the costume feminine Holland asks above all things apparently a very flat, narrow chest, surmounting enormous hips, and Volendam is no exception to this fashion rule.

The invariable black "best waist" of the older women is usually brightened by a square yoke of lighter color and material, and the dark apron or overskirt is topped by six inches or more of gay plaid or bright colored band worn over an underskirt of dull blue striped or black material and uncountable petticoats.

About the throat a collar formed of many rows of heavy dark red coral beads is fastened by huge silver clasps, and the number of rows, the size and quality of the beads are matters for feminine pride.

Long hair is not the only glory of woman in Holland, save perhaps at Marken. It is usually hidden and at Volendam is cut quite close and entirely covered by a tight fitting thick black silk cap concealed beneath the snowy white lace.

The younger girls, from the tiniest toddler to the young meisje, old enough to wed, wear dresses and caps the exact counterpart of their grave mothers, no less full of skirt or narrow of chest, but much gayer in color. A group of tiny maidens in a stiff breeze on the dike resemble nothing more than a swarm of butterflies.

His Only Escape

There is a story often told to illustrate the manner in which President Lincoln was besieged by commission seekers. Hearing that a brigadier general and his horse had been captured and the general taken to Richmond, he asked eagerly about the horse.

"The horse," exclaimed his informant. "You want to know about the horse?"

"Yes," said Lincoln. "I can make a brigadier any day, but the horse was valuable."

To this John Russell Young, in his memoirs, adds a similar tale. He was calling upon Lincoln one day at the White House.

"I met So-and-so on the steps," he remarked.

"Yes," replied the president. "I have just made his son a brigadier."

"A general!" exclaimed Mr. Young in astonishment.

"Yes," said Mr. Lincoln, with a great weariness, "You know I must have some time for something else."

The Clever Baby

Nodd — You say your baby doesn't walk yet? Mine does. Same age too. Your baby cut his teeth yet"

Todd — No.

Nodd — Mine has — all of them. Your baby talk?

Todd — Not yet. Can yours?

Nodd — Great Scott, yes!

Todd (desperately) — Does he shave himself or go to the barbers?

ADVERTISEMENT FROM PAGE 3

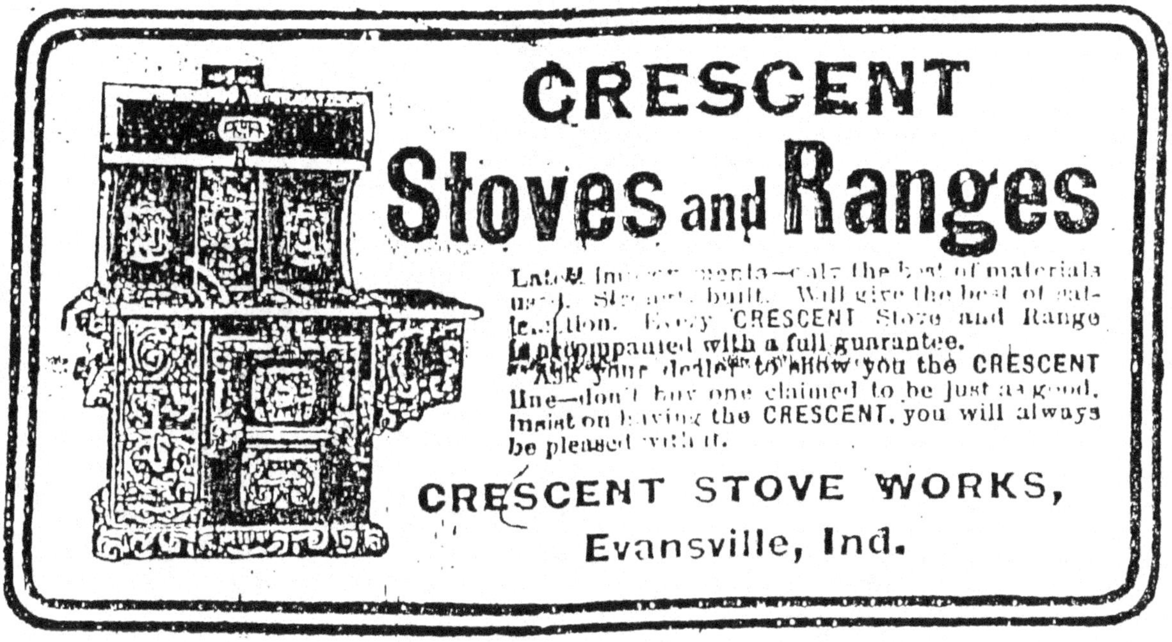

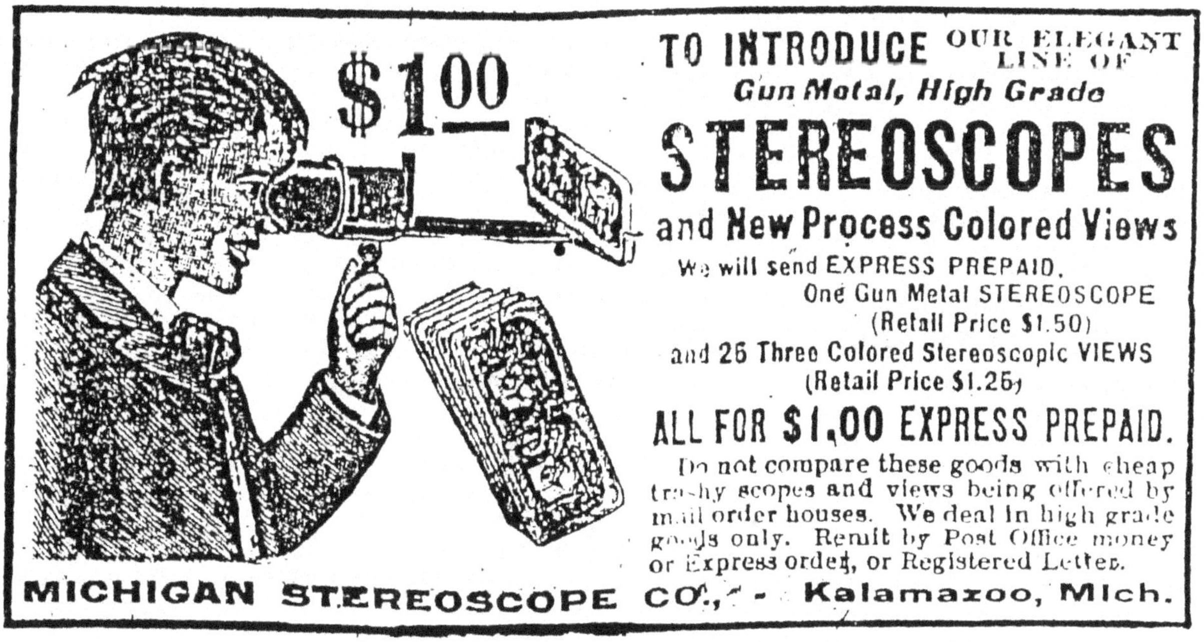

ADVERTISEMENTS FROM PAGE 3

[Page 4]

SUBSCRIPTION RATES

One Year (in advance) . . . . 50¢
Six Months . . . . 30¢
Three Months . . . . 20¢

A rate of 75¢ will be charged when paid in advance.

A simple X mark opposite your name indicates that your subscription has expired, while a XX shows you are in arrears.

CORRESPONDENCE

Correspondence is solicited, but every contribution should be accompanied by the name of the author to insure its publication. This rule will be insisted upon.

FRIDAY, SEPTEMBER 13, 1907

Still the cry goes up for more houses.

President Roosevelt is to visit Nashville October 22.

Oklahoma will vote on her new constitution next Tuesday.

The supreme court began its East Tennessee session at Knoxville this week.

There may be enough of the pie brigade to renominate President Roosevelt, but it will take more than that to elect him.

There is much comment in the press over the alleged fact that William R. Hearst made a sensible speech on Labor Day.

Congressman Theodore Burton has been nominated by republicans to run against Tom Johnson for mayor of Cleveland, Ohio.

By the way it takes almost as long to get the battleship fleet off to the Pacific as it would to build a new one. The date now fixed for its departure is December.

The president's latest stunt is to advise women to ride a-saddle. This will involve putting on the breeches. What is to become of us poor men? Whither shall we fly?

An honest newspaper can no more afford to allow public abuse to go unchallenged without lifting its protest than a sentinel can passively allow his camp to be invaded by the enemy while all are aslep.

The Madisonville Democrat is exercised over an alleged combination between Carmack and Bob Taylor. The story, however, is about as probable as Bryan's nomination of Roosevelt for the presidency.

Col. Newell Sanders has abdicated his claims on the position of republican national committee in favor of Congressman Hale. The Evans crowd was probably afraid the Hon. Nathan Wesley would change front again.

THE HERALD has set the pace in more things than its subscription price. It now sees people lined up under the white banner of temperance who once fought tooth and nail against it while THE HERALD led the forlorn hope. Imitation is the truest flattery.

The courts have awarded title to the state of Tennessee to about 10,000 acres of fine land which was left west of the Missisippi [sic] by a change in the river's channel. The land is estimated to be worth a million, and it has been suggsted that the proceeds be added to the school fund.

THE DORTCH LAW

Some interest has been aroused in legal and political circles by a recent decision of Chancellor McConnell sitting at Athens, holding that the Dortch secret ballot law does not apply to McMinn county, and, incidentally that it does not apply to but four of the largest counties and the city of Jackson. This interest has been augmented somewhat by the fact that the decisions, if upheld by the supreme court, would result in the voting of ignorant and criminal negroes with greater facility in the centers of population, a result that it is figured would redound to the advantage of republicans and, in a corresponding ratio, to the disadvantage of democrats.

We say these are possibilities as suggested by Judge McConnell's view of the case, but we find as a matter of fact, that there is a general opinion among lawyers and laymen that the supreme court will view the matter in altogether a different light. Several incidents are pointed out as a basis for this opinion, among them: The suggestion that while McConnell is one of the ablest equity judges in the state, he has not been very consistent in his opinions touching politico-legal questions; the fact that the act of 1897, extending the Dortch law to civil districts of 2500 population and over, was ignored in the argument and decision of the case before Judge McConnell; and to the further fact that the supreme court has almost uniformly upheld all laws having for their purposes the extension of the area covered by the Dortch or secret ballot laws.

Another feature of the chancellor's remarkable decision is the holding that the Dortch and registration laws are not necessarily co-extensive, as has been the uniform supposition of people generally. But while, unlike our (and Dave Rhea's) friend Miller, we are not a very profound student of constitutional law, we incline to think that here again the chancellor will be reversed.

There are provisions of both the Dortch and registration laws that do not mean anything if they do not mean that these laws are complementary to each other. At least that is the way the matter appears to an unsophisticated member of the common herd. Rhea county has been mentioned among others as likely to be effected by Judge McConnell's opinion in the McMinn county case, but we suggest that our readers wait for the final returns before becoming alarmed.

THREE IN ONE

The Rhea County News has been (is to be) removed from Spring City to Dayton. This makes three weekly newspapers for Dayton and at least one of them is bound to go to the wall or all three suffer in the struggle for existence. Three papers are one too many for Dayton. A

"third paper" in Augusta has just gone to the boneyard, likewise the recently organized "State" in Montgomery. In these days of rising prices and keen competition, in the newspaper world it takes a mighty good city to support a "third paper" and our opinion is that the Rhea County News would have done better to have remained in Spring City. — Cleveland Journal and Banner.

The Journal and Banner is in a position to speak with authority on the "third paper," having seen the experiment tried in its own town, a community much older and wealthier than Dayton. If it wouldn't go there, what may be expected here?

A newspaper is a business proposition and yet, it is something more than that. Every true journalist owes a duty to his community and to his profession that he cannot properly perform if his field is so crowded that graft and mendicancy are made necessary to eke out a mere existence.

THE HERALD holds no exclusive franchise on the local newspaper situation, and desires none. But it has occupied the field several years and has endeavored to make good. It flatters itself that it has the confidence and respect of the community it has striven so faithfully to serve. It is grateful to friends and the public for their generous patronage and will continue to be. Meanwhile it [is] not making any preparations to move hence.

CHURCH MAKES REPLY
TO THE PUBLIC —

The First Baptist church of Dayton is not inclined to engage in newspaper controversy, and less so when the subject is scandal. Neither is it in the habit of offering explanation or apology for its actions as a body. But a recent publication by some one over the signature of Miss Kate Knight was so glaringly false and scurrilous as perhaps to merit passing notice.

This church will not turn aside from its purpose to engage in a war of words with a woman though it may not accept as true her story of injured "innocence." It begs to suggest that she may not always have known what was being said in the community respecting her "fair name." For instance, a former pastor who then, as now, was on intimate terms with her family, is alleged to have warned some of his members against allowing their daughters to associate with Miss Kate.

"Rev. W.L. Head" held a series of meetings in the church last winter, and later, on the insistance of Bro. Knight and others, he was called to the pastorate. During the delay incident to procuring a lodging place he and his family accepted an apparently earnest invitation to stop with the Knights. He has since regretted this step.

Long after the Heads had moved elsewhere Miss Knight sprung a sensation by alleging that two months previously she had been insulted by Rev. Head in her home. Not many people believed the story, which seemed so inconsistent with physical facts and circumstances. It was hard to reconcile her profession of maidenly purity and "innocence" and her story of wrong with the facts that she swallowed the alleged insult with sweet complacency, continued to treat him as the favored guest of the family, insisted on having him and his wife visit at her home after their removal and capped the climax by offering her hand at church in request for his prayer that she might lead a better life.

Having been indirectly reproved in a sermon and learning that her pastor's wife had mentioned to a friend about what she regarded as Miss Knight's indiscreet conduct in receiving the attentions of a well-known gentleman the incredible story of alleged insult was started and a clever scheme was planned to run the preacher out of town before the matter could be looked into. But the scheme failed. The church was called together and a committee, consisting of W.A. Howard, Wm. Whitlock and A.H. Rollins, was appointed to investigate. It is perhaps sufficient to say that this committee was satisfactory to all concerned.

It began its work by hearing Miss Knight's statement which was followed by the testimony of several persons who were acquainted with [the] facts. The preacher's reputation wherever he had lived was gone into and found above reproach. A report was made that the committee did not believe Miss Knight's story, and the report was unanimously adopted by the church. Members of the committee state that they did not wish to humiliate Miss Knight and her family by making public all the testimony taken, but state further that when the "vindication" process is begun in the courts they will be there with the proof.

Regarding the "disarming" and "cursing" episode it is unnecessary to multiply words. The story is too ridiculous to dignify with denial. Too many good people know the facts — to be exactly the opposite of the published statement. However, it is about as true as the other allegations. "Yet he (Head) is pastor of the First Baptist church." Yes, the church is prospering, as it has not in recent years. Baptist churches choose their own pastors (probably the greatest sin of the First church). They have no power to punish anybody, and want none. They reserve the right, however, to withdraw fellowship when it is so clear, as in the instance in controversy, that fellowship no longer subsists.

The pastor of the First Baptist church is a man of God, and in the fear of God is doing a great work. He has the confidence of his flock and of those who know him. While the tongue of slander has been busy, he has given little heed to it and has continually grown in favor with God and man. Like his Master, he has refused to return reviling for reviling, even declining to prosecute the man who assailed him with violence and vituperation on the public street. He has likewise counseled leniency and moderation in dealing with those who are persecuting him and the church when his brethren have called them to account.

Now, while the church, of course, would not presume to advise Miss Kate, it might suggest that she is not benefited by those who flaunt her name in the public prints to gratify their own spleen.   BY ORDER OF CHURCH

The Independent League

That's a funny name to give to a concern that belongs — body, boot and breeches — to W. R. Hearst.

If you want to enlist under Mr. Hearst, for better or for worst, until death do us part, run right along and join the Independence LEAGUE.

Of all leagues, it is the least independent. — Wasson's Jeffersonian.

ADVERTISEMENTS FROM PAGE 4

[Page 5]

BITS OF LOCAL INFORMATION

Concerning Our People, Business and Progress in the County and Town

T.C. Bailey spent Monday in Chattanooga.

D.R. Bolen is recuperating at Rhea Springs.

Brack Blevins was in Chattanooga yesterday.

W.O. Hudson spent Monday in Rockwood.

Raleigh Hood, of Coulterville, was here Monday.

J.W. Hudson was in Chattanooga last Saturday.

Col. W.L. Givens visited Decatur Monday.

Dr. J.L. Goodwin was here Monday from Spring City.

Miss Claudia Frazier was out from Washington Monday.

H.C. Bridgman was up from Chattanooga Wednesday.

Capt. M.H. Clift, of Chattanooga, was here Tuesday.

Hoyal Robinson, of Lorraine, was in the city yesterday.

Rev. D.V. Culver is here from Loudon, Ky., for a few days.

T.F. Robinson, of Washington, spent the week with relatives here.

Mrs. J.L. Henry spent last Sunday at Harriman, the guest of her daughter.

W.A. Ault was in Cincinnati the first of the week laying in his fall stock.

Hon. and Mrs. J.W. Lillard, of Decatur, were guests of relatives here yesterday.

J.T. Crawford and F.E. Robinson were in Atlanta Monday, returning Tuesday.

F.M. Marler and daughter, Miss Lizzie of Carp, were shoppng in the city last Saturday.

Prof. A.V. Woodworth, of Grandview, attended the teachers instiutte here last Saturday.

Capt. S.J.A. Frazier, of Hill City, was the guest of Col. R.N. Gillespie Wednesday evening.

James Abel, of Jamestown, N.Y., was the guest of relatives here for a few days the past week.

T.J. Robinson and Oscar Smith, of Evensville, and R.H. Locke, of Meigs county, were here Monday.

Jno S. Leuty was here from Maloney Tuesday, and while in the city remembered THE HERALD.

Miss Imogene Woolen has as her guests Misses Ethyl and Moera Holloway, of Tallahassee, Fla.

Cunnyngham and Locke, Spring City attorneys, were attending to legal business here yesterday.

Ozias Jordon, an old and respected citizen of Graysville, died suddenly Wednesday, of heart disease.

Twelve or fifteen new students have entered the county high school since our last paper was printed.

Baby won't suffer five minutes with croup if you apply Dr. Thomas' Electric Oil at once. It acts like magic.

N.D. Reed, E.M. Williamson, W.B. Kelly and sheriff J.S. Frazier attended the fair at Kingston this week.

Belgian hares for sale, any size you may want, at prices to suit. F.E. Denton, City Transfer.

Mr. and Mrs. C.L. Locke were out from Washington last Saturday to attend the institute and witness the colt show.

Ladies when in need of a pair of first class shoes see the new fall line of Dorothy Dodd shoes at J.F. Henninger's.

Rev. W.L. Head attended a family reunion at the residence of his father near LaFayette, Ga., the first of the week.

Mrs. Joe Goodman and Mrs. King Redmon have returned to Paris, Ky., after visiting the family of Mr. G.W. Woolen.

Regulates the bowels, promotes easy natural movements, cures constipation — Doan's Regulates. Ask your druggist for them. 25 cents a box.

DeWitt's Little Early Risers are good for anyone who needs a pill. They are small, safe, sure little pills that do not gripe or sicken. Sold by Crawford & Robinson and W.F. Thomison.

ADVERTISEMENT FROM PAGE 5

Samuel Mynatt, Samuel Frazier, I.K. Brown, J.L. Wyrick and Isaac Byrd were all here from Washington Monday.

Dr. E.E. Folk, editor of the Baptist and Reflector, preached at the First Baptist church last Sunday morning.

Sheriff Jas. S. Frazier returned Wednesday evening from Red Boiling Springs where he had been recuperating.

Impure blood runs you down — makes you an easy victim for organic diseases. Burdeck Blood Bitters purifies the blood — cures the cause — builds you up.

J. Scott Young, for several years a citizen of Dayton, but now in the government service at Norfolk, Va., was the guest of old friends here this week.

Doan's Ointment cured me of eczema that had annoyed me a long time. — Hon. S.W. Matthews, Commissioner Labor Statistics, Augusta, Me.

Prof. W.H. Taylor was here from Graysville last Saturday to attend a meeting of J.W. Gillespie Camp. Prof. Taylor is one of the youngest old men of the county.

DeWitt's Carbonized Witch Hazel Salve is good for boils, burns, cuts, scaldi and skin diseases. It is especially good for piles. Sold by Crawford & Robinson and W.F. Thomison.

The old Federal soldiers of Rhea, Meigs and Bledsoe counties are making merry at their annual reunion at Graysville today. A number of people from Dayton are in attendance.

SALESMAN WANTED to look after our intertest in Rhea and adjacent counties. Salary or Commission. Address, The Victor Oil Company, Cleveland, O.

Recorder J.L. Godsey visited his wife, who is in very poor health, at the home of her parents at Jefferson City, this week. He reports that Mrs. Godsey shows no improvement.

The way to get rid of a cold, whether it be a "bad cold" or just a little one, is to get it out of your system through your bowels. Nearly all Cough Cures, especially those that contain opiates, are constipating. Kennedy's Laxative Cough Syrup contains no opiates and acts gently on the bowels. Pleasant to take. Sold by Crawford & Robinson and W.F. Thomison.

Misses Ruth Aiken, of Cleveland, Carrie Coulter, of Sale Creek, Alie Pace, of South Pittsburg, and Arvazene Abel, of Soddy, were all guests of Miss May Abel within the past week.

FOR SALE. — A second-hand Standard organ, in good condition, excellent tone, fine walnut, adjustable stool. Wholesale price, $85, will accept $25, if sold before Sept. 17, 1907. Call on or address,   F.M. MORRISON,
Dayton, Tenn.

B.F. Mealer, proprietor of the Mineral Springs Hotel, has some of the tallest corn ever seen hereabouts, and it didn't grow in a jug either. Mr. Mealer brought it from Panama last spring and planted it in his garden. The stalks are from fifteen to twenty feet high, but have no ears to speak of — only small shoots.

SALE NOTICE

In obedience to a decree of the chancery court at Dayton, Tenn., made in the case of Laura A. Gillespie vs T.G. Gillespie, I will on the 16th day of Oct. 1907, at the residence of said Laura A. Gillespie in Spring City, Tenn., sell to the highest and best bidder the property in said decree discribed, being the household and kitchen furniture including the personal property and furniture of every kind in the house and about the premises, as set out in said decree at the date thereof.

Also all the right, title, claim and interest which T.G. Gillespie had at the date of the original decree in said cause under the will of Lucinda Gillespie, or by descent, purchase or otherwise in and to the lands known as the Abernathy lands, situated in the Second Civil District of Rhea county, Tenn., which said land is described in a deed made on the 30th of March, 1885, by J.C. Abernathy and sons to T.G. Gillespie and Lucinda Gillespie, registered in the register's office of Rhea county, Tenn., in Book P, pages 202-3-4, as may be necessary to pay the amount of said decree with interest and cost. Said sale will be for cash in hand, and the real estate in bar of redemption. This 12th day of Sept. 1907.

J.F. DOSSON,
Special Commissioner

ADVERTISEMENT FROM PAGE 5

NEW FIRM

Euclid Waterhouse has purchased a half interest in R.J. Coulter's undertaking business and the firm hereafter will be Coulter & Waterhouse.

The new firm has purchased a nice casket wagon and other modern fixtures which makes their large stock entirely complete. They are having fitted up a nice office, sample room and chapel, and will soon have the nicest undertaking establishment in the county.

Off for Jamestown

A party consisting of Mr. and Mrs. Euclid Waterhouse, Mr. and Mrs. J.M. Gass, Mr. and Mrs. R.P. Abel and Trustee J.T. Crawford left yesterday for the Jamestown exposition and other points east.

Several of the party will visit New York, Niagra Falls, Washington and possibly Boston before returning. The trip will last from two to three weeks.

ADVERTISEMENTS FROM PAGE 5

ADVERTISEMENT FROM PAGE 5

[Page 6]

THE LION AND
THE MOUSE.

BY CHARLES KLEIN

A Story of American Life Novelized From the Play by
ARTHUR HORNBLOW

COPYRIGHT, 1906, BY G. W. DILLINGHAM COMPANY.

Origin of "Hip, Hip, Hurrah!"

A London paper, answering a question as to the derivation of "Hip, hip, hurrah!" printed the following excerpt on the subject from the London Tatler of 1832: "During the stirring times of the crusade the chivalry of Europe was excited to arms by the inflammatory appeals of the well known Peter the Hermit.

While preaching the crusade this famous zealot was accustomed to exhibit a banner emblazoned with the letters H.E.P., the initials of the Latin words, 'Hierosolytma Est Perdita' (Jerusalem is destroyed). The people in some of the countries which he visited, not being acquainted with Latin, read and pronounced the inscription as if one word — Hep. The followers of the Hermit were accustomed, whenever an unfortunate Jew appeared in the streets, to raise the cry, 'Hep, hep, hurra,' to hunt him down and flesh upon the defenseless Israelite their maiden swords, before they essayed their temper with the scimiter of the Saracen."

The Corn Cultivator

If the corn cultivator undergoes as much improvement in the next few years as it has in the past, it will almost be a white shirt job to plow corn. The dustless feature should be next given attention by makers. — Farmer in Iowa Homestead.

Finicky

"Cleanliness is a prime factor in successful chicken farming," said an expert. "Keep the runs clean, dry, cheerful and your hens will do their duty by you nobly. In fact, to make hens lay well it is almost necessary to carry neatness to the finicky point — to be as finicky as the old lady with the aquarium.

TENDRILS

Moving Parts Which Are The "Brains of Plant Life"

There are two classes of plants which are incited by Man's presence to describe certain definite movements. One class, the sensitive plants, retract their leaflets as we approach them, as if they resented any attempt at closer intimacy, while the other class, comprising all those vines which develop climbing organs called tendrils, will reach out toward us if we place our hands in contact with them and will even use a finger as a support to climb upon. We know that these tendrils will wind just as readily about a twig or a grass stem, but as one feels these sensitive strands multiply their encircling coils about one's fingers there almost seems to be established between us and the vegetable world a more intimate relationship than existed before.

Tendrils are indeed capable of exhibiting faculties and going through evolutions more wonderful perhaps than many of us realize. It is only after we have seen them at work, testing with their sensitive tips the objects they come in contact with, apparently considering their suitability as a support and then accepting or rejecting them, as the case may be — it is only then that we realize how justly they have been called the "brains of plant life."

The thoroughness with which these wandering tips explore their surroundings is illustrated by an instance I observed in a grapevine tendril. A cherry branch whose leaves had been variously punctured and scalloped by insects hung near the tendrill, and a particular leaf had just one small hole in its blade, not over three-sixteenths of an inch in diameter. So careful had been the exploration of the leaf's surface that this one small hole had been discovered by the tendrill, which had thrust itself nearly three inches through the opening. — Harper's Magazine.

The Sleep of Horses

When the horse sleeps, it is said that one ear is directed forward, why is not known. A writer in the English Mechanic thinks this is to guard against danger, being a survival of its originally wild habits.

ADVERTISEMENTS FROM PAGE 6

[Page 7]

The Colt Show

Dayton had a colt show last Saturday. And while it was gotten up on short notice much interest was manifested. The town was full of people and quite a goodly number of fine colts were on exhibition.

In the afternoon the crowd assembled on the public square and a committee, consisting of W.C. Godsey, W.A. Templeton and J.W. Clouse, was selected to inspect the colts. After a careful survey of the field the prize ($10 in cash) was awarded to W.P. Thomison Jr.

Considerable interest is now manifested among Rhea county farmers in improving the strains of their live stock and their methods of farming.

[NOTE: the remaining articles on this page were testimonials about cures for a number of illnesses and are not being included here. B.J.B.]

ADVERTISEMENTS FROM PAGE 7

ADVERTISEMENTS FROM PAGE 7

[Page 8]

RHEA SPRINGS

Selected as Place for Confederate Reunion Oct. 3

CONFEDERATE REUNION

The J.W. Gillespie Camp at its meeting on the 7th inst., fixed Rhea Springs as the place for the annual reunion of the Rhea and Meigs county ex-Confederates, and Thursday the 3rd day of October, as the time. All are cordially invited. Rhea county will furnish commissary supplies.

The foregoing simple announcement was handed in for publication by the commander of J.W. Gillespie camp.

Once more! The scattered fragments of the armies of Lee and Jackson, Johnson and Beauregard, Hood and Early and Kirby Smith, are to meet again and renew the comradship and rehash the scene of other days ere passing over the river to rest under the shade. But few are left. The inexorable march of time has kept in continual progress until a large majority of the heroes of the lost cause have broken ranks, and have met and overcome their last enemy to be conquered.

By all means let there be reunions as long as there remains as many as two of the grizzled veterans left. Let's accept the kindly invitation to attend and augment the joy of the occasion. Let's show ourselves worthy sons and daughters of noble sires by vieing with each other in making their last days their best days and in making them feel that they have not lived in vain.

SPECIAL MEETING

Dr. J.B. PHILLIPS, who is to join the pastors of the city in a series of special revival meetings, is one of the most eminent evangelists in the state of Georgia. He is also pastor of one of the leading Baptist churches of Macon, in that state.

The meeting will begin next Sunday evening and will probably alternate between the First Baptist and First Avenue Methodist churches. All Christian people are invited to join in the movement for a cleaner, more righteous Dayton. Services will be held each afternoon and evening.

A special choir of the best local talent is being trained to sing at the services during the meeting, which it is planned to make very spiritual and morally uplifting.

Teachers' Institute

The teachers' monthly institute met Saturday and there were only a very few teachers absent. The meeting was an extraordinary one considering that it was the first of the year's work.

Opened by devotional exercises by Prof. A.V. Woodworth. Next was a very interesting paper read by Miss Myrtle Boyd, "Number Work in the Primary Grades." It was something original and that made it more practical than some things we have had before.

Prof. Frazier made a talk on the "Added Responsibilities of a Teacher." He gave a number of good suggestions in regard to keeping of school rooms, order and recitations.

A lecture to the teachers on how and why the institutes should be made interesting was made by Prof. Fooshee.

Miss Mabel Fair read a paper on Domestic Science which was heartily enjoyed by all present.

Prof. Stephens, with his usual eloquence, thrilled the whole audience with his speech on "Loyalty to our Schools," a question which should be considered by all teachers.

Then came the organization of the institute proper. Prof. Stephens was elected chairman for the coming year, and Miss Virginia McPherson secretary. Prof. Lowry was elected on the program committee with the privilege of selecting two others for the same committee. Another committee was elected to select instructors for the reading circle work for the coming year.

Collection, adjourned 2:30.

The Unembellished One

Drape me with a fig leaf,
  said Prudery.
Decorate me with epaulets,
  said Mediocrity.
Clothe me in the robes of
  righteousness, said
  Sin.
Deck me with the garments
  of innocence, said
  Vice.
Put sincerity's gown upon
  my shoulder, said
  Desire.
Place the crown of fidelity
  on my brow, said
  Disloyalty.
Cover me with the drape-
  ries of love, said
  Lust.
Give me the staff of tole-
  rance, said Perse-
  cution.
Adorn me with the cloak of
  liberty, said Tyrann.
Beautify me with the dress
  of duty, said --?--.
Garb me with the rain-
  ments of humility,
  said Pride.
Then Truth said: Let me
  be naked and una-
  shamed. —
            From Life.

INDEX

www.ingramcontent.com/pod-product-compliance
Lightning Source LLC
Chambersburg PA
CBHW080617270326
41928CB00016B/3093